Donum Dignitatis
The Catholic's Guide to Miscarriage

Elizabeth Petrucelli

Nickdow Maher Publishing

Parker, CO

Copyright © 2022 by Elizabeth Petrucelli

All Rights Reserved. No part of this book may be reproduced, distributed, or transmitted, in any form or by any means, including photocopying or stored in a database or retrieval system, without the prior written permission of the author; except by a reviewer who may quote brief passages in a review to be printed in a magazine or newspaper.

Nihil Obstat:	Father Luis Granados, S.T.D.
	Censor Librorum
Imprimatur:	+Most Reverend Samuel J. Aquila, S.T.L.
	Archbishop of Denver
	Denver, Colorado, USA
	November 18, 2022

Published by Nickdow Maher Publishing
Library of Congress Control Number: 2023909097
ISBN: 978-0-9851713-5-3
Edited by Melanie Saxton
Cover Design by Elizabeth Petrucelli
Cover Photo by titoOnz – iStock

All Scripture contained herein is from the Revised Standard Version, Second Catholic Edition ©2006 by the Division of Christian Education of the National Council of the Churches of Christ in the United States of America. All rights reserved.

DISCLAIMER:

This book's aim is to serve as a guide. **It is not intended to serve as medical advice.** The author accepts no liability or responsibility for any loss or damage caused or thought to be caused by reading and/or acting upon the information in this book and recommends that you consult a healthcare professional for medical advice or to ask questions regarding the details contained herein.

May the Lord bless you and keep you.

CONTENTS

Foreword by Kelly Breaux – Red Bird Ministries............1

Introduction..7

Chapter One: What is Miscarriage?............................13

Chapter Two: Managing Miscarriage..........................18

Chapter Three: Experiences and Warning Signs...........31

Chapter Four: Waiting in Prayer.................................39

Chapter Five: Options for Your Baby's Body................43

Chapter Six: After the Miscarriage..............................53

Chapter Seven: Causes..61

Chapter Eight: Where is My Baby?..............................66

Chapter Nine: Suffering..72

Chapter Ten: Others Who Grieve................................87

Chapter Eleven: Sharing Your Loss.............................93

Chapter Twelve: Other Things to Consider.................101

Chapter Thirteen: Re-entering Society........................105

Chapter Fourteen: Pregnancy After Loss.....................112

Chapter Fifteen: Imago Dei...118

Author Bio 123

Resources...126

Bibliography..128

Donum Dignitatis
The Catholic's Guide to Miscarriage

FOREWORD

It is no secret that the Catholic Church has been a leader in science and medicine at various times throughout history. For centuries, the Church has gone into the margins to create and meet the unmet needs of the world. From the education system to the hospital system, the Church leads the way in innovation. Over two millennia, Christian doctors and nurses, inspired by the example and teaching of Jesus Christ, have been at the forefront of efforts to alleviate human suffering, cure disease, and advance knowledge and understanding. The Catholic Church is filled with many holy men and women that went before us, paving the way to proclaim the gospel at every chance they could, even in the medical community. In addition to promoting peace and unity, they loudly and proudly elevated life and the dignity of the human person. Through a Christian lens, science and medicine have advanced. But the culture of life that the church sees itself through and built into the western world has been destroyed by the works of evil.

As grateful as I am for the church's role in advancing science and medicine while caring for the human body, I am confused about where we are today. Worldwide, millions of miscarriages are reported every year, but the church has very little understanding of this issue. Miscarriage is still a taboo subject to talk about. Catholic leaders are reluctant to discuss the subject, and families are not prepared to deal with the heartbreaking waters of grief when learning their baby has no heartbeat. When we fail to address the pain, grief, and loss experienced during a miscarriage, we cannot effectively advocate for life. The work we do will fall on deaf ears with those who don't value life. Still, some faithful Catholics only advocate for life from one side of the aisle, by stopping and eradicating abortion. In order to truly value life, we must present a clear message on both sides of the aisle, including the wanted life lost in the womb. In the first few weeks of life, a baby is valued, and his/her dignity remains intact. If we do not acknowledge loss appropriately, do we truly value life? There is nothing worse than death. It was not a part of God's original plan, and it was for this reason that Jesus Christ had to redeem it.

Throughout church history, there are many saints who have spoken through their wounds to proclaim God's glory. Some saints had a heart for the broken, despite having no personal experience to draw on. It shocked me to learn that St. Catherine of Siena is the patron saint of miscarriages. I knew little about St. Catherine's life. The little I knew led me to focus mostly on her fiery spirit, telling Pope Gregory XI to get back to Rome. She was certainly opinionated, rather extreme and dictatorial in her language, and yet she held no official position of authority. She wasn't a doctor, a nurse, or a psychologist. She had no letters behind her name, and her only qualification for ministering to women experiencing miscarriage was love. Love was present within her, a love derived from Christ.

There was no denying that she was a force to be reckoned with. St. Catherine of Siena said, "Be who God made you to be, and you will set the world on fire." And indeed, she did. Through my own journey of loss and finding healing within the Catholic church, my heart became alive. How does one become a doctor of the church with such sass? It is only reasonable to conclude that she allowed herself to be led by divine inspiration throughout her life. It wasn't enough for her to wait for the world to change before taking action. In action, she allowed herself to be led by God.

As one of only four women doctors of the Church, St. Catherine of Siena is revered for her deep devotion to God and role as a spiritual mother. One of the most significant works of mystical theology is "The Dialogue," which continues to be studied and revered today for its insights into the nature of divine love and mystical experiences. She is considered one of the most important mystics in Church history. How did this great saint, who wasn't a mother of loss, spend most of her life ministering to women who suffered a loss? St. Catherine had a gift for serving others and was willing to do so. It was her passion to care for the mind, body, and heart of those who suffered miscarriages or developed illnesses during their pregnancy. During these difficult times, she was considered a prayer warrior for these women, for their recovery, and for the repose of their child's soul. Those who are suffering from miscarriages or face the prospect of one continue to call upon the intercession of St. Catherine of Siena.

While we wish to emulate the holiness of Saint Catherine of Siena, we cannot duplicate her precisely. However, we can emulate her perseverance and fortitude in eradicating society's errors and correcting those who err. We can imitate her tireless ways. One of those errors that the Western Church has allowed to manifest itself in society is a disconnect from the idea that the Church is a place of healing for people. There is a widespread perception that bereavement and miscarriage support should be dealt with by medical professionals only. Less than 5% of church parishes hold space for grievers, and many families must seek healing in the secular world. It is a world that is dominated by science and medicine and does not see Christ as the healer.

In our work with Red Bird Ministries, we work with many families who have experienced miscarriages, and many share they have not found a safe place to land in the church after a loss has occurred. In most cases, funerals or burials are not offered. Many parents are unaware that their children can be named. Meeting men and women with similar stories, feeling so lost and alone after losing a child, saddens my heart.

When suffering enters into our families' lives, and the search for healing begins, the church should be the first place they turn. Our failure to extend our arms wide will lead them to search elsewhere. While grieving my own losses, I have never quite understood why the church did not come to my family's aid when I needed her most. Losing a child, regardless of whether it occurs during pregnancy or after childhood, requires the church's attention and compassion and most certainly accompaniment. It is only possible for the medical community to treat the body and mind. Our souls and our hearts require the attention of the church. Only the Divine Healer can heal our deepest wounds, and the loss of a child calls for this kind of healing. Some wounds are so deep they require two touches, just as with the blind man.

In Donum Dignitatis, we learn so much about the nature of miscarriage and how common it is. In addition, the author brings the reader to the foot of the Cross to illustrate that miscarriage is not a heavy period. Miscarriage is the birth of an immortal soul. It is important to treat the body of that child with dignity and respect. As a part of the healing process, the church plays a vital role in providing closure to families. The parish should offer a proper funeral and burial for the child. If we leave healing to the medical community in a post-Christian world, our faithful families will be forced to handle sacred life, like medical waste. Educating ourselves is the first step to educating others. By elevating all life, including those that we wanted, we can continue to be innovators and change the culture of death to one of life.

When a child leaves the womb for Jesus, tears and mourning are appropriate responses. There is nothing more terrible than death, and that is why Jesus had to defeat it. Each day, I pray for the faithful Catholic community to continue validating life, especially for those little babies who were wanted.

St. Catherine of Siena,

Humble Virgin and Doctor of the Church, in thirty-three years you achieved great perfection and became the counselor of Popes. You know the temptations of mothers today as well as the dangers that await unborn infants. Intercede for me that I may avoid miscarriage and bring forth a healthy baby who will become a true child of God. Also pray for all mothers, that they may not resort to abortion but help bring a new life into the world. Amen.

O Saint Catherine of Siena, God our Father enkindled the flame of holy love in your heart as you meditated on the Passion of Jesus His Son. Moved by His grace, you devoted your life to the poor and the sick, as well as to the peace and unity of the Church. Through your intercession, may we also come to know the love of Jesus, bring His compassion to all, and work for the unity of His Church. We ask this in Jesus' Name and for His sake. Amen.

God, You caused St. Catherine to shine with Divine love in the contemplation of the Lord's Passion and in the service of Your Church. By her help, grant that Your people, associated in the mystery of Christ, may ever exult in the revelation of His glory. Amen.

Kelly Breaux, President/Co-Founder
Red Bird Ministries Inc

INTRODUCTION

In April 2010, I experienced my first miscarriage. It was one of the most devastating experiences of my life. I kept a journal of my experience to help me process my grief and published it as my first book, *All That is Seen and Unseen; A Journey Through a First Trimester Miscarriage*. I won't share my entire story here; you can read it in my first book, but the experience of losing my second child Ruby, led me to decades of helping others through the loss of their child, whether in pregnancy or the newborn period.

It was truly an honor to assist families through their darkest moments, but there were many atrocities I observed. These atrocities were often preventable and caused more harm than good. Nurses and doctors seemed oblivious to the hurt they caused through a lack of compassion or describing miscarriage as "just a heavy period," implying there should be nothing more to the experience than a minor inconvenience. I discovered that even with the very wanted babies who die during pregnancy, secular society has little to no respect for the unborn.

It became apparent that families needed to be armed with more information, preferably at the miscarriage diagnosis. *It's Not Just a Heavy Period; The Miscarriage Handbook* was the answer to this problem. When families are informed, they have a better understanding of the process of miscarriage, and this helps with their grief. This book is used in some hospitals and clinics nationwide.

I learned an immense amount about miscarriage after experiencing it myself. For one, I didn't realize how common it was, even though I worked as a doula for over five years before I experienced my own miscarriage. I wrongly assumed my horrific experience was out of the ordinary. I assumed my doctor's lack of compassion for what I was feeling was "just a bad day for him." Now I understand that it's very common, and many doctors fail to recognize the personal crisis in their patients. Through conversations and meetings at clinics, I learned that doctors also lack resources. When these doctors became educated, they changed their practice and, in turn, could better help grieving patients.

I didn't just grow in my knowledge of the miscarriage experience; I also grew in my Catholic faith. I was raised Catholic, so you would call me a cradle Catholic. Like many cradle Catholics, I was unaware of the depth of my Catholic faith, and I had little insight into the teachings of the Church. When I lost Ruby, I considered myself a devout Catholic. However, if I was honest with myself, I was a mediocre Catholic. Losing Ruby really challenged my faith because I became angry at God. Why would He bless me with a child, only to take her away? How could He Will this child to death? Will I see my child again? These are questions I had, as do many women experiencing the loss of a child.

I believe the loss of Ruby was just the beginning of learning the love of our heavenly Father and all that He wants for us. I had little understanding of death, both physical and spiritual, nor an understanding of the inherent dignity of the human person. I had experienced suffering in my life but knew nothing about the actual benefits to suffering. Ruby's loss threw me into suffering I had never experienced before; a darkness I never knew existed.

I wasn't suffering very well. I forced myself to attend Mass, but I sat in the pews with my arms crossed, like a child having a tantrum. How many souls in purgatory could have been saved through my suffering if I had only offered it to God? I am ashamed now to think about it, but I learned that not many people know how to suffer. This isn't hard to believe when we live in a world doing everything possible to erase discomfort and suffering. I was never offered advice on how to use my suffering, and even more so, I had no idea how to bring God into my suffering. Why wasn't the Church teaching me this?

About nine months after my loss, I began to reemerge from the depths of suffering. I'd like to say there was an "ah-ha" moment for me, but there wasn't. I'd also like to say that I read some books that taught me how to suffer, but I didn't. I entered a new normal, and it was like I was starting over. Yet God was calling me. It was as if He was saying, "Follow Me, Elizabeth, I need you to share." So, I began to research and study.

I knew very little about the dignity my child deserved, though somehow, I knew that her short life was significant and that she should be treated with the same dignity as any human who had died. I felt called to name her and didn't realize that it was that is was recommended that we give her a name. It wasn't until I sought some guidance from my priest that he shared that we should name her. He also recommended we celebrate her short life, though I didn't know how, and he didn't provide the way. Unfortunately, this seems to be quite common within the Church.

I discovered that the priest who encouraged me to name Ruby was a rarity. For the Church to be so pro-life, there were very few resources for miscarriage and stillbirth. I would find that many priests were ill-equipped to offer guidance, and there was little follow-up to the guidance offered. One priest even shared that if all women knew what the Church could do in terms of rites for their unborn children, it would overwhelm the parish. I quickly saw that as Catholics, we were falling short. We have a fantastic platform, if you will, for leading the way in providing dignity. Why were resources lacking?

With all I had learned, I saw a need — a need for dignity, not just for the baby who died but for the families experiencing the loss. Women were being left to grieve in silence, torn between what they felt in their hearts with what society was telling them. Women were told to get over it because they were "barely pregnant." Too many babies were being flushed down toilets or placed in planters. These locations are not dignified "resting places" and go against Catholic teaching. Where does a Catholic find Catholic teaching as well as information on the physical aspects of miscarriage? **In this book.**

We lost another child in 2015, a little boy we named Augustus Jude. Augustus had a fatal condition called Full Triploidy which is not compatible with life and increases the risk of early preeclampsia and other conditions in the mother which could turn fatal. We did not know of his diagnosis until after he was born and had testing conducted, but it explained some of the strange symptoms and issues I struggled with during my short pregnancy.

I remember the day the genetic counselor called me to give me the testing results. Her first words to me, other than confirming my name on the phone were, "I don't know how this information will be helpful for you, but the pregnancy was a boy, and it had Full Triploidy." She said this in the most condescending voice and called him an "it." She must have had no idea how painful it was for her to tell me that I should have no feelings whatsoever about the child who died inside me because he wasn't "normal." It was as if she was saying, "See, most babies who die in the first trimester have genetic anomalies." Without testing, we have no idea why babies die in the first trimester, especially after we see their heartbeat.

We saw Gus's heartbeat several times. It was beautiful, and I hold his "thump, thump, thump" sound in my head like a favorite piece of music. But what this genetic counselor didn't realize was that she held the key to my peace. Not only did she confirm the sex of my baby, whom I knew was a boy the moment I conceived him, but she also showed me just how special I was. My grief began to lift from that moment, and I recognized I was chosen.

God chose me to be the mother of this child, a child who would never take an earthly breath. A child whose life would begin and end in the darkness of my womb. He would never feel pain or hate. He only experienced love. Love is all he knew then and all he knows now. I was chosen to be this child's path to ensoulment, and instead of anger at God like I had with Ruby, I had acceptance and knew what to do.

The genetic counselor proved a point though, that she did not see the dignity of the human person. She only saw numbers and statistics. Her sole purpose was to help create "perfect" children and convince families, whose genetics would not likely produce a perfect child, to prevent, abort, or use reproductive technologies to bypass God's design. Dignity was lacking.

My son deserved better, and he received it. I had a Catholic midwife who encouraged me to give birth instead of having surgery to remove him. We had our priest come to our home to minister to us during this difficult time. Unfortunately, as time passed, surgery became necessary, but the midwife acknowledged the dignity of my son's existence and helped ensure he was buried in a proper place. I remember sobbing over the fact that he would need to be removed in pieces, his tiny body torn apart and placed in a jar. This did not seem dignifying but was the way in which his birth needed to be completed.

The midwife helped ensure his remains made it to the cemetery. This was a very different experience than with Ruby, whose remains were discarded with hospital trash. The Catholic faith of this midwife was integral in the process and what I needed for closure. Our archdiocese was involved, and our son was buried in Mount Olivet with other babies whose mother's wombs served as tombs. Our pastor held a beautiful commendation ceremony for him and us. This helped tremendously in our grief, and the information in this book is designed to help you in your grief.

Biblical scholars and holy priests have helped me write this resource based on Catholic teaching and Tradition along with the Holy Spirit. This book is not my opinion. It's a summary of different documents and teachings of the Church. Some of these teachings are very hard to accept and seem harsh. It was hard for me to accept and hard for me to write, but it was necessary. *Donum Dignitatis: The Catholic's Guide to Miscarriage* mimics *It's Not Just a Heavy Period; The Miscarriage Handbook*, but contains all things Catholic. This book will guide you, as a Catholic, through the proper understanding and handling of your miscarriage. The content is very sensitive and blunt.

Your child deserves the dignity that any other living human would. Your child lived even if only inside of you. The information here will help you learn and understand what to do when a baby dies during pregnancy.

Dominus Vobiscum.

You formed my inmost being; you knit me in my mother's womb. – PSALM 139:13

CHAPTER ONE: WHAT IS MISCARRIAGE?

Your baby was designed by God. Your baby was known by God. This wasn't a chance happening. This was purposeful, even if you are reading this book because your baby has now died. Your baby had purpose and meaning and was a living, growing person. As Catholics, we believe that life begins at conception, also known as fertilization. It may surprise you to know that the scientific community also defines fertilization as "the development of a human being." The moment the egg and sperm become one, a new life has formed. This is a new living human being with their own genetic structure separate and unique from its parents.

Science cannot answer the question of when the soul enters the body or is united with the body; however, David writes in Psalm 51:5 that he was a sinner from conception. In order for anyone to be a sinner, one must have a spirit or soul. We cannot demonstrate the soul is not infused at conception; therefore, it is most probable that your child has a soul at conception. A soul must be created, "*for as the body apart from the spirit is dead.*" (Jam 2:26)

The term miscarriage is actually not a medical term though we often hear it presented by medical providers. Unfortunately, the medical term for miscarriage is "spontaneous abortion," which can be quite upsetting. Please note that the term abortion (used below) does not refer to the deliberate and purposeful termination of human life, but merely refers to the "naturally occurring" death of the embryo/fetus or more commonly referred to as "baby or child." Below are the definitions and terms you may hear when medical providers reference your pregnancy and baby.

Following this chapter, the book will use the term miscarriage to describe pregnancy loss before 20 weeks gestation. These terms are merely presented here due to some medical providers using medical terms. Hearing these terms may be quite difficult for you, but these terms are not meant to cause you any pain. They are only utilized as assigned terms.

Definitions

- Zygote (conception to implantation)
- Embryo (conception to 8 weeks)
- Fetus (after 8 weeks)

Other medical terms used:

- Tissue
- Products of conception

A **miscarriage** is defined in the United States as a pregnancy loss prior to 20 weeks gestation[1]. After 20 weeks gestation, pregnancy loss is defined as a stillbirth. Miscarriage is the most common form of pregnancy loss and occurs in approximately one in four pregnancies.

A **spontaneous abortion** or **spontaneous miscarriage** occurs when the baby is not viable, which means they are unable to survive, or when the baby is expelled/

born before 20 weeks gestation. It is usually just called "miscarriage."

A **complete abortion** or **complete miscarriage** occurs when the baby and all products of conception (placenta, gestational sac) have emptied from the uterus. Cramping and bleeding typically subside quickly following a complete miscarriage. An ultrasound is used to confirm.

An **incomplete abortion** or **incomplete miscarriage** occurs when only parts (baby, gestational sac, placenta) have passed, but other parts remain in the uterus. Bleeding and cramping continue to occur, although a woman may experience a decrease in cramping and bleeding. However, after a period of time, the bleeding and cramping reoccur and can be more intense.

A **missed abortion** or **missed miscarriage** occurs when the baby dies but is not expelled from the uterus. Often, the mother discovers this during an ultrasound, and no fetal heartbeat is detected for the proper gestational age, or no further growth is seen when comparing previous ultrasounds.

An **inevitable abortion** or **inevitable miscarriage** occurs when there is dilation or effacement of the cervix and/or a rupture of the membranes (water breaks). It most commonly occurs with back pain and/or abdominal pain. These contractions cause the cervix to soften and open. If this continues, the baby (embryo or fetus) will be born.

A **threatened abortion** or **threatened miscarriage** occurs when there is vaginal bleeding accompanied with cramping, but the cervix is not softening or opening. The mother may experience abdominal pain, lower back pain, and bleeding that is pink, brown, or red.

A **blighted ovum** occurs when the fertilized egg implants, but no baby develops or the baby stops developing. In some cases, a yolk sac may develop inside the gestational sac, but no baby forms. This can cause confusion as to whether you were really "pregnant." Catholics believe life begins at conception. A new life did form, but a genetic problem took place, and proper development did not occur. The body may reabsorb a blighted ovum, but not in all cases.

A **chemical pregnancy** occurs very early and results in bleeding around the time a woman misses her period. Many women do not know they were pregnant and may notice heavier bleeding and cramping, possible clots, and suspect she is/was pregnant. A chemical pregnancy does not mean you weren't pregnant. It is a complication that occurs soon after conception. HCG levels (pregnancy hormone) may rise enough to show a positive pregnancy test, but shortly after, the levels decrease due to the baby's death.

An intrauterine fetal demise occurs when the baby dies inside the uterus after 20 weeks gestation; however, some clinicians use this term for babies who die during pregnancy in the second trimester.

A **live miscarriage** occurs when the baby is born and shows signs of life, such as a heartbeat, movement, or breathing. Even very early babies (7 weeks gestation and older) have been seen in their gestational sacs with a heart beating or moving. The baby may survive for seconds, minutes, or hours, but no medical intervention can be performed due to how early the baby was born. This is not a medically recognized occurrence, but many women report this.

Note:
These last three are different variations of pregnancy and pregnancy loss.

A **molar[2] pregnancy** occurs in about 1 in 1000 pregnancies. It is also called a hydatidiform mole, a medical term meaning a fluid-filled mass of cells (mole = a mass of cells; hydatid = containing fluid-filled sacs or cysts). A molar pregnancy rarely involves a developing baby and occurs due to a genetic error during fertilization. An ultrasound would reveal grape-like clusters with placental parts. Because a placenta forms, HCG is secreted, and a positive pregnancy test can be seen. Unfortunately, no baby develops. Only abnormal tissue grows (and grows very rapidly) in the uterus. A molar pregnancy can be cancerous but is usually non-cancerous. It is also referred to as gestational trophoblastic disease (GTD).

A **partial molar pregnancy** occurs when there are abnormal cells and a developing baby. The baby usually has severe defects and is quickly consumed by the abnormal tissue.

Molar and partial molar pregnancies require follow-up procedures/treatment, and many doctors recommend waiting at least one year before attempting to conceive again (although this varies).

An **ectopic pregnancy** occurs when a fertilized egg implants outside the uterus. The most common location is implantation in the fallopian tubes, but a fertilized egg can implant in other locations, although this is extremely rare. This is an extremely dangerous situation that can result in maternal death. Treatment options are discussed in a later chapter. If time permits, your Catholic bio-ethics group should be consulted before proceeding with treatment. Many women have been counseled incorrectly by their priests due to the complexity of this pregnancy complication.

God did not make death, and he does not delight in the death of the living, For he created all things that they might exist.
— WISDOM 1:13-15

CHAPTER TWO: MANAGING MISCARRIAGE

When you learn your baby has died, it can be a time of confusion and grief. Often, women struggle with understanding their options for delivering the baby. There may be a period of disbelief and uncertainty with contemplation on whether or not the diagnosis is correct. "Maybe it's too early" is a very common thought. If you are experiencing an ectopic pregnancy, please skip to that section in this chapter below. The following paragraphs explain the medical and scientific calculations for pregnancy to help you have a better understanding.

The medical community calculates pregnancy weeks by a woman's last menstrual period (LMP). This means that two (2) weeks are added to the gestational age of the baby. But not all women ovulate exactly 14 days after the first day of their periods. Many Catholics chart their fertility and are aware of when ovulation takes place, but the secular medical community often discounts women's charts and knowledge of their own bodies. Some online calculators can help determine the gestational age of the baby using the ovulation/conception date.

By the time a woman can confirm pregnancy with a pregnancy test, or even through a blood test, she is likely around four weeks pregnant. Chemical pregnancy loss occurs at this time if it is going to occur. A woman may receive a positive pregnancy test as early as eight or nine days following ovulation, but by fourteen days past ovulation (the most common time to experience a positive pregnancy test), the test could now be negative due to a chemical pregnancy loss.

Women often look to the lines on the pregnancy test to determine the viability or success of a pregnancy. Some positive pregnancy test lines are faint; others are very dark. This can vary from day to day for many reasons, time of day, for instance, how diluted the urine might be due to water intake, and, of course, the sensitivity of the pregnancy test in detecting HCG. Some are very sensitive, and some are not. Not all of these tests share what level of HCG the test detects in their information packets. A line is a line. If you see one, consider yourself pregnant. The darkness of the line is not an indicator of viability or non-viability.

Even if we know when ovulation occurred, implantation is much harder to determine. Implantation can happen early or late, and the timing of implantation affects gestational age. For the purposes of this chapter, we are discussing late implantation and the risks associated with determining early gestational age. Doctors use crown-to-rump[3] (CRL) length to determine gestational age in early pregnancy. There are other markers to consider, such as the gestational sac (shape and size) as well as the yolk sac (shape and size), but, again, we're going to talk specifically about CRL. Late implantation can affect the gestational age, making the baby appear smaller or less viable based on perceived gestational age.

This is why it's important to understand that if you are very early in pregnancy, your baby and/or your baby's heartbeat might not be detectable on an ultrasound. HCG blood levels typically need to be above 1000mIU to see a gestational sac[4] and/or fetal pole utilizing transvaginal ultrasound (not abdominal). Even if the HCG blood levels are high enough, the baby's heartbeat might not be detectable until six weeks and three days, or later.

Waiting to find out may be difficult during this already stressful time, but this is the time when mistakes are most frequently made. Bleeding can be considered normal during very early pregnancy; therefore, bleeding alone is not a good indicator of an impending miscarriage. Bleeding coupled with cramping is also not a good indicator, especially very early in pregnancy; however, if you previously saw your baby's heartbeat and now a heartbeat is no longer detected, it's very likely the baby has died.

It is imperative that vaginal (not abdominal) ultrasound be coupled with blood tests to ensure that the baby is, in fact, deceased before beginning any form of miscarriage treatment/management. Your medical provider would note no visible heartbeat on ultrasound and falling HCG levels. A minimum of two ultrasounds performed one week apart would best ensure you are not delivering a viable baby prematurely if using medical/surgical management of miscarriage (see below).

After being told your baby has died, it can be difficult to know how to proceed. You have many choices available to you, but most often, medical providers offer little to no options, or rather, they do not present anything as optional at all. The options for delivering your baby include expectant management, medical management, and surgical management (D&C: Dilatation and Curettage or D&E: Dilatation and Evacuation). These options are for confirmed miscarriage (baby no longer has a heartbeat) and blighted ovum; however, miscarriage is often misdiagnosed, which can lead to inducing a miscarriage or performing a D&C on a living baby. Please consult your medical provider if you believe you are experiencing a miscarriage. **This information should not be substituted for medical advice.**

Expectant Management

Delivering naturally at home (expectant management of miscarriage) can be a viable option for many women. Sometimes it can be very healing to wait and have your baby at home; however, there are some risks. It is important to understand that no research explains when the miscarriage will start or how long it will take to complete. The miscarriage could begin shortly after diagnosis or take days, weeks, or even months to begin.

Risks associated with expectant management:

- Hemorrhaging (excessive bleeding)
- Incomplete miscarriage (not everything is expelled and may require surgery)
- Infection
- Could take days, weeks, or months to begin

Benefits of expectant management:

- May help with closure
- May allow you to see/hold your baby
- May allow testing of your baby

This option may lead to the need for an unplanned or emergency D&C[5] (surgical intervention – see below) due to an incomplete miscarriage. It is important to monitor bleeding when your miscarriage process begins and watch for infection over the following weeks. If you see clots larger than the size of an egg or a plum, you should call your medical provider or proceed to the nearest emergency room.

Always have a driving adult with you in case you need emergency care. Take your temperature regularly and if you experience fever, contact your medical provider right away. You may also experience moderate to intense pain. Your medical provider can prescribe pain medications to help. Always call a medical provider if you believe you are having a miscarriage.

Medical Management

Using medication to induce the miscarriage (medical management) is a good option if you need to plan when your miscarriage will happen. The miscarriage will usually occur within a few hours after the first dose, although this varies greatly depending on the gestational age of the baby. Sometimes utilizing this method can take several doses over several days and still lead to the need for a D&C (surgical intervention).

This option is usually offered as a take-home treatment; however, that does not mean this method is low risk. For pregnancies beyond 14 weeks, it is recommended that a hospital induction occur for safety reasons. Be sure that your doctor checks (ultrasound) and then double checks that the baby has died before choosing this option.

The medication most commonly used to induce miscarriage is Cytotec®, also known as misoprostol.

Risks associated with medical management:

- Intense cramping
- Hemorrhaging (excessive bleeding)
- Incomplete miscarriage (could lead to surgical intervention)
- Accidental abortion (medication taken without confirming the death of baby)
- Infection

Benefits of medical management:

- May help time the miscarriage
- May help with closure
- May allow you to see/hold your baby
- May allow testing of your baby

This is not a complete list of risks. The risks are greater if you have had prior uterine surgery such as a cesarean section, surgical abortion/termination, or other uterine surgeries. The medication can be taken sublingually (under the tongue), orally, or vaginally. It is most often given orally with early miscarriage and vaginally with second-trimester miscarriage, although it can be administered either way.

Side effects from the medication may include abdominal pain, cramping, nausea/vomiting, low-grade fever and/or chills, skin rash, and diarrhea. There are differing statistics on how effective this method is, with numbers ranging from 60%-90%.

Sometimes during hospital inductions for miscarriage, a foley bulb is used to help the cervix dilate. This is part of the induction process and may include the use of Pitocin® — a synthetic hormone that stimulates uterine contractions. This may happen with babies who are between 16 and 20 weeks.

If you deliver in a hospital, bonding time with your baby should be encouraged. While at home, you will have as much time as you would like with your baby. If you are at home and need time to plan the final resting place for your baby, you may temporarily place your baby in your refrigerator (the freezer is not recommended). It is not wrong to place the your baby's remains in the freezer; however, if the remains are thawed, the decomposition process speeds up rapidly. This is more of a concern for larger babies (over 12 weeks).

Surgical Management

A **D&C** for miscarriage (short for dilatation and curettage) is an outpatient surgical procedure. The procedure differs from a D&E (dilatation and evacuation), explained later. A D&C is most commonly performed in a hospital or a same-day surgery center. However, some doctors can perform this procedure in their office (reserved for very early miscarriages), and it can be quite painful. Before choosing this option, be sure your doctor checks with an ultrasound and then double checks one week later to ensure a viable baby will not be surgically removed.

For the procedure, you are usually given a sedative and general anesthesia. Your legs are often placed in stirrups once on the operating table. This can feel awkward because your legs may be placed there while you are still awake. If this process sounds like it may be uncomfortable for you, talk with the surgeon prior to the surgery.

Once you are anesthetized, the surgeon will place a speculum in your vagina and begin to artificially dilate the cervix with instruments. The cervix is dilated just enough to insert a curette (an instrument used for scraping). The surgeon will then scrape the lining of the uterus to remove tissue. In some cases, a vacuum aspirator is needed and may be referred to as "suction curettage," which scrapes the lining of the uterus and sucks out tissue. This procedure does not allow your baby to remain intact, but you have some options for burial and testing (see chapter 3).

The procedure usually takes anywhere from 15 to 30 minutes. It is rare for this procedure to require an overnight stay. You will also likely be given an antibiotic to prevent infection.

A D&C should be conducted using ultrasound to help guide the surgeon. Consult with your surgeon to ensure this is used. Failure to use the ultrasound can result in uterine perforation and uterine scarring.

Risks associated with the D&C:

- Adverse reaction to anesthesia medication
- Hemorrhage or heavy bleeding
- Infection in the uterus or other pelvic organs
- Perforation or puncture of the uterus
- Laceration or weakening of the cervix
- Scarring of the uterus or cervix (Asherman's Syndrome – see below)
- Incomplete procedure which requires another procedure to be performed

Benefits of the D&C:

- It can be scheduled
- Can provide enough tissue for testing (if you choose this)
- May bring closure or relief if you have been waiting for the inevitable miscarriage

The **D&E (dilatation and evacuation)** is generally performed for miscarriages over 12 weeks gestation. The difference between a D&C and D&E procedure is that during a D&E, the surgeon dilates the cervix and then uses a grasping instrument (forceps) to remove the baby. Because the uterus is not dilated enough to remove the entire baby all at once, the baby must be removed in pieces. Once the baby is removed, a vacuum or curettage procedure is used for the remaining tissue in the uterus.

While this is a very effective and viable option, some families would like to see and hold their baby, possibly take pictures of and with their baby, receive handprints/footprints from their baby, wash their baby, dress their baby, provide dignified services/blessings, and bury or cremate their baby. Some of these options are not available with a D&E.

Seeing your very early baby may be traumatizing. Always be sure you have someone with you while you are miscarrying. Some doulas specialize in supporting families through loss. These doulas may be called bereavement doulas, perinatal loss doulas, or baby loss family advisors. A search on the internet should reveal a doula in your area.

Ectopic Pregnancy

Ectopic pregnancy is a potentially life-threatening condition and presents a seemingly impossible decision. The treatment presents several moral issues for Catholics, and unfortunately, few priests are well-versed in this issue. The National Catholic Bioethics Center has a paper[6] on ectopic pregnancy for doctors, priests, and laypeople to consult. Much of what they present is listed below.

Currently, there are four treatments for an ectopic pregnancy. If the baby has a heartbeat, this will limit the treatment. It is important to consult with your Diocesan Catholic Bio-Ethics team or the National Catholic Bio-Ethics Center (NCBC) along with your priest. The four treatments are: expectant management, removal of part or all of the fallopian tube, ligating the fallopian tube (if that is the baby's location) and removing the baby from the tube, and finally, the administration of methotrexate.

Expectant Management (morally permissible) is warranted in some cases and has been successful. Expectant management requires waiting for the ectopic pregnancy to resolve on its own, which means through the natural death of the baby and the body reabsorbing the tissue. This is a viable option with a patient and caring medical provider and has been successful[7] at reducing the other risks associated with surgical management. Women must be under near constant doctor supervision.

Removing part or all of the fallopian tube (morally permissible) would indirectly cause the death of the baby. This falls under the principle of double effect. The action (removal of the fallopian tube) is a good effect to preserve the mother's life. The baby dying is the bad effect, one not chosen by the mother. This is the principle of double effect. This is morally permissible because nothing is being done to directly kill the growing baby. The removal of the fallopian tube or segment of the fallopian tube results in the death of the baby, which is not the same as taking a medication directly that kills the baby. Loss of fertility can result from this procedure.

Ligating the fallopian tube and removing the baby from the tube (impermissible) directly kills the baby. This is not morally permissible by the majority of Catholic ethicists. The risk to the mother does not outweigh the life of the baby. Using this procedure also damages the fallopian tube, which increases the risk that an ectopic pregnancy would reoccur in the fallopian tube. Loss of fertility can result from this procedure.

Administration of methotrexate (possibly impermissible) is the most common treatment for ectopic pregnancy; however, the Magisterium has not resolved the controversy of this treatment. Methotrexate is a drug used in cancer treatments, rheumatoid arthritis, and psoriasis. It helps these conditions by slowing the growth of cells. In an ectopic pregnancy, it slows the growth of the rapidly dividing cells (the baby/embryo), in turn, killing the baby. The body then reabsorbs the baby. This is not a quick process and takes several weeks to complete. If the baby has already died, the use of methotrexate is irrelevant and would not be needed. Yet, many medical providers utilize methotrexate under these circumstances. It is also used in "pregnancy of unknown location."

There are risks to using this drug, including severe birth defects in future pregnancies. Subsequent pregnancy should be delayed at least three months or longer following the use of methotrexate, which means doctors usually recommend contraception. Using contraception for this reason is not morally permissible and is contrary to Catholic teaching. Practicing abstinence is warranted in this situation and is permissible by the Church. It is not an offense against the conjugal right.

What does the Catholic Church teach on this pregnancy complication? The Church doesn't have a teaching directly related to ectopic pregnancy, but the Church does teach that the direct killing of the innocent is always wrong, and there is widespread debate, even among Catholic theologians, on what that actually means.

This is why the treatment of ectopic pregnancy puts a woman in an impossible position.

It's important to note that, according to Catholic teaching, all persons have dignity and value. Babies in the womb have the same value and right to life from conception until natural death as any other human person. The life of the mother has no more value than the life of the unborn baby. We are all equal in the eyes of our Creator from the moment of our existence (conception). This is a difficult concept for many, especially within secular society.

Our secular world determines the value of one's life in a very different way than our Creator, such as physical characteristics/looks, productivity in society, age, etc.

For more information:
Visit the Vatican's website and read *Donum Vitae, Dignitatis Personae*, the *Instruction on Respect for Human Life in its Origin* and *the Dignity of Procreation; Replies to Certain Questions of the Day by the Congregation for the Doctrine of Faith.*

Note for RH Negative Women

If you are Rh-negative and experience a miscarriage, you may need the Rh immunoglobulin injection[8]. Please talk with your medical provider. If your body produces antibodies due to the baby being Rh-positive, this can cause serious complications during a later pregnancy.

Asherman's Syndrome

Asherman's Syndrome is a scarring of the uterus that can lead to recurrent miscarriage/infertility and uterine dysfunction. One of the best ways to prevent Asherman's Syndrome is to use medical management for your miscarriage. While it can be more painful, it can prevent future complications due to scar tissue.

If you choose to have a D&C, it is highly recommended that your surgeon conduct an ultrasound-guided D&C instead of a blind D&C. Using the ultrasound while performing this procedure helps the surgeon see where they need to use the suction instead of just blindly scraping inside of your womb and possibly damaging more areas. This also helps reduce the chance of needing a repeat procedure for failing to remove all the products of conception.

Following the procedure, your surgeon may place a balloon or stent inside your uterus for approximately two weeks. The balloon may also be referred to as a splint. This is not the standard of care; however, some surgeons utilize this technique. The splint is placed, and a catheter runs out of your vagina, which allows bleeding and fluids to come out. Placing this splint inside your uterus may help prevent the layers of the uterus from binding to each other, causing the scar tissue known as Asherman's Syndrome.

Another therapy that your surgeon may utilize is estrogen therapy. This therapy may be combined with the splint therapy above. Estrogen therapy lasts for approximately 2 to 4 weeks. It is used to encourage healing by slowing progesterone production, thus slowing the building of the lining of the uterus while your uterus heals. There are risks to utilizing estrogen therapy, including blood clots, so you will need to discuss the benefits versus the risks with your medical provider.

And after you have suffered a little while, the God of all grace, who has called you to his eternal glory in Christ, will himself restore, establish, and strengthen you. - 1 PETER 5:10

CHAPTER THREE: EXPERIENCES AND WARNING SIGNS

What You Might Experience

There is no single way to experience a miscarriage. Everyone's experience will be different. The most common description of a miscarriage by a medical provider is, "It's just a heavy period." While some women may experience their miscarriage in this way, most women do not. Your miscarriage experience will also depend greatly on the gestational age of your baby.

From conception to week four: Women are discovering they are pregnant earlier now than at any other time in history. This results in women knowing they are experiencing a pregnancy loss very early. Fifty percent of all pregnancy losses occur at this stage of pregnancy. A chemical pregnancy is an extremely early pregnancy loss and may result in a heavier period. Most commonly, women report that their periods are a day or two "late" with more clots, heavier bleeding, and stronger cramping. Because a chemical pregnancy is lost so close to when a woman would usually start her period, many women don't even realize they are pregnant and suspect a pregnancy only due to how different this period was from others in the past.

From weeks four to eight: Women have reported their miscarriage as painful and much more than just a heavy period. Women experience heavy bleeding and cramping, large clots, and the passing of gray tissue. Women have taken pictures of the tiny babies they have birthed, although most women will only see gray tissue or tiny fragments of the placenta. Once the heartbeat is seen, less than 5% of women miscarry at this stage of pregnancy.

From weeks eight to 13: Women have reported their miscarriage as similar to labor, having a contraction pattern that is intense with their pain ending at the birth of their baby. Some women report feeling their baby slide through their vagina and fall into the toilet, bath, or into their hands. Many of these babies are fully intact, and some are still within their gestational sacs.

From weeks 13 to 19 (second trimester): This experience of miscarriage is far from "just a heavy period." Women usually experience mild cramping that leads them to seek medical care, but the cramping progresses into labor with patterned contractions and heavy bleeding. They may feel their water break and experience a release of amniotic fluid before or after bleeding begins. The physical pain ends at the birth of their baby. They often go to the emergency room and learn they are having a miscarriage. Some of these babies are born alive but are too small and fragile for any life-saving medical intervention. At this gestation, the family can see and hold their tiny baby. One to five percent of miscarriages occur at this stage of pregnancy. Your breasts may produce milk following a second-trimester loss.

Note:
In the United States, pregnancy loss at 20 weeks gestation is called a stillbirth. However, in the United Kingdom, it is not called stillbirth until 24 weeks gestation.

Warning Signs:
If you experience any of the below signs, please contact your medical provider immediately or visit your closest emergency room.

- Vaginal bleeding that soaks more than one pad per hour.
- Passing blood clots that are larger than a golf ball.
- Sudden swelling of hands or face, vision changes, or pain in your upper right abdomen below the ribs.
- Fever over 100.3 degrees Fahrenheit.
- Swollen, red, painful area on your leg (a sign of a blood clot).
- Signs of vaginal or uterine infection: redness, swelling, pain, and/or foul-smelling drainage from the vagina.
- Inability to urinate.
- Intuition tells you something is wrong.

Lactation

Your body is prepared to breastfeed your baby by the fifth month; however, some women report producing milk with a loss as early as 12 weeks. Your body doesn't know your baby has died and may produce milk, even if you have never breastfed a baby before. Although some women have found it healing, this can be both physically and emotionally painful.

If lactation occurs, you will typically feel engorgement sometime between days two and five following the birth of the baby. Engorgement is a painful swelling of your breasts due to milk production. Many women describe this feeling as "breasts like rocks."

You have two options:

- Drying up
- Donating breastmilk

Drying Up

It doesn't matter what option you choose. Do not feel guilty if you choose to dry up. Many women will bind their breasts and take ibuprofen to relieve some of the pain; however, binding is no longer recommended and may carry the risk of developing clogged ducts and mastitis (breast infection).

It is recommended that you wear a bra and use cold packs and raw cabbage leaves. Place the raw or frozen cabbage leaves in your bra-like breast pads. Wear them until they wilt. You can replace these several times a day. Cabbage leaf extract or Cabo Cream© can be purchased to help dry up breastmilk. Please note that it is important not to use heat on your breasts during the time of engorgement as it can increase pain and swelling.

You will also want to avoid any nipple stimulation, such as letting the shower water spray onto your breasts. Medications and natural remedies like herbs and peppermint can help dry up breastmilk. Please consult an herbalist and discuss these options with your medical provider.

You may need to pump or hand express a little milk to relieve some of the pressure. If this is the case, use an electric pump, manual pump, or hand express for two to three minutes after your milk starts flowing. Pumping or expressing for much longer may stimulate milk production and delay the drying-up process. Any milk collected can be stored in the freezer, poured down the drain, or donated to a milk bank (if you qualify). You may also send your milk to a company to have it preserved and turned into jewelry.

While you are waiting for your milk to dry up (which can take several days to weeks), breast pads can help absorb any leaking. Most stores carry disposable breast pads, but reusable cloth pads can also be purchased online or at breastfeeding specialty stores. If the thought of going to the store to purchase these items is painful, ask someone else to pick them up for you.

Donating Breastmilk

Milk donation is quite a commitment; however, some women find this process very healing. Many babies will benefit from your donated breastmilk, including babies who are very sick, premature, dying, or have mothers who cannot produce enough milk or any at all and rely on donations like yours to feed their babies. This can be a living gift to another baby and their parents.

If you choose to donate, it's best to have an electric breast pump. Even though your baby died, your insurance company should provide you with an electric breast pump. However, this is not always the case, and it can be very painful if you don't qualify because you don't have a living baby. You can ask your local hospital if you can borrow or rent one, but there are private businesses that will rent pumps if the hospital doesn't have one available. You can also purchase a pump at any store that sells them.

There are two ways to donate breastmilk, via a milk bank or through private donation, also referred to as milk sharing.

Utilizing a human milk bank is very safe. This involves applying and being accepted by a milk bank. At the time of this publication, there are 33 human milk banks in the United States and Canada. Visit https://www.hmbana.org/ to locate a milk bank near your area. You do not have to be near a milk bank to donate. Many will accept your donation from other states. You will need to apply and qualify as a donor. There are several steps in this process:

- Call or email an inquiry to the milk bank.
- Participate in an eligibility interview.
- Complete a lifestyle history and medical review.
- Complete a medical release form which will need to be signed by your doctor.
- Consent to and receive blood tests for HIV, HTLV, Syphilis, Hepatitis C, and Hepatitis B.

There is also a specific way that milk is collected, and the sterilization of parts must be adhered to. In addition, you will need to agree to the human milk bank guidelines in their information packet, which describes the acceptable use of over-the-counter medications, drugs, alcohol, smoking, caffeine, herbs, and vitamins.

If you do not qualify for a milk bank donation, you can privately donate your milk. There are several private donation websites and groups available on the internet. Human Milk 4 Human Babies and Eats on Feets are two very popular milk-sharing groups. In these groups, you may be paired with a family or several families to provide milk. It can be very gratifying because, in many cases, you develop a relationship with the family. At the very least, you usually receive a picture of the baby receiving your milk, which can be comforting. Milk sharing; however, does have some safety risks. Always meet in a public place when exchanging milk with anyone.

You will need storage containers and/or breast milk bags if you want to pump. Pump every three to four hours. The milk collected can be added to any milk already stored in a refrigerator, but do not pour warm milk into frozen milk containers. You will receive instructions on how to pump and store milk from the milk bank if you are qualified to donate.

Some women have found it comforting to pump every few hours and throughout the night because it's something that any mother would do if she had just had a baby. Others do not want to wake up and pump, so they only pump during the day. If your goal is to pump long-term, you will still need to pump during the night to maintain a milk supply.

It is important to really listen to your own desires. You do not have to do any of this if you do not want to. Even if you agree to donate milk and then decide it is too hard or too much, you can stop at any time. If you choose to stop though, you will need to slowly wean by increasing the time between pumps and decreasing the time you pump. If you stop cold turkey, you may become engorged and experience pain or develop clogged ducts and/or mastitis (breast infection).

If you had been pumping every three hours for about 20 minutes, try pumping every four to five hours and only for 15 minutes. Continue to decrease the pumping length and increase the time between pumps over several days. You will dry up within a few days to a few weeks. The goal is to gradually decrease pumping and not just stop all at once.

If you have questions or concerns about drying up your milk or donating, contact your doctor or hospital's lactation consultant or find a local lactation consultant to assist you. You can also create a keepsake with your milk through an organization that preserves milk. It is a wonderful memento that can remind you of your baby and the pregnancy.

Warning Signs:
Hard, painful lumps in your breast or armpit area. Any sore, painful, reddened area in your breast or armpit area is a sign of impending mastitis. This can quickly lead to feeling flu-like symptoms and fever. Contact your medical provider if you experience any of these symptoms.

Have no anxiety about anything, but in everything by prayer and supplication with thanksgiving let your requests be made known to God. And the peace of God, which passes all understanding, will keep your hearts and your minds in Christ Jesus. – PHILIPPIANS 4:6-7

CHAPTER FOUR: WAITING IN PRAYER

Since the recommendation is to wait before proceeding with medical management or surgical management of miscarriage (see early chapters), waiting to begin the miscarriage can be agonizing. Some women find it helpful to meditate on the First Sorrowful Mystery: The Agony in the Garden as they wait. Rushing to "get this over with" could be deadly for your baby if it's just too early to see a heartbeat. Therefore, turn towards God. It is very easy to turn away from God during this time, but don't.

When our babies die, whether inside or outside, God doesn't find joy in our pain at all. Remember, death was never a part of God's original plan (see Genesis 1-3). We were to live in Paradise with God, but due to the sin of our first parents, we suffer in this world. One day, we shall be in Paradise. The death of a baby is very hard. Burying our children was not something we were made for. Take a deep breath, open your heart to mourning, entrust your baby to God's care, and allow your body to let go.

As you wait for your miscarriage to begin, with every cramp and every wipe of blood, you will wonder, is this it? Is this the beginning of the end? This itself will bring on feelings and emotions, such as "What do I do?" "I'm not ready for this." "Please Lord, save my baby!" Ask God to give you strength in these moments and offer up your suffering (see Chapter Nine).

The Diocese of Columbus has approved the "Chaplet of Hannah's Tears," which may bring you some solace. You may also find the novena for "Mary, Undoer of Knots" extremely helpful. Do your best to unite yourself to Christ in His suffering, but tell your husband and reach out to a priest if you feel like you are entering desolation or despair. Desolation is emptiness or a lack of God, and despair is a complete lack of hope. These come from the devil. It is in these times that we must cling to God.

We must ask for his love and help through all we are experiencing. This is an excellent and appropriate time to go to adoration. Many parishes have perpetual adoration. A search on the internet will help you find a local parish, or your parish may already have set times to go. Bring your rosary and some tissues. Ask God for peace no matter what happens.

As you wait, you may search for areas you can control. Don't make big decisions, or even little ones, like cutting your hair. It will be a short-lasting relief and might be a bad haircut. Surrender your perceived control to God.

Once the miscarriage is over, you may find a bit of peace and feel relief. This does not mean you didn't love your baby. Usually, the grief comes soon after. Accept the feelings you do have, and do not judge yourself based on the experiences of others.

Miscarriage Preparation

An inevitable miscarriage may give you time to prepare. Below is a list of items you may find helpful to have on hand. Heaven's Gain is an organization you can find online and purchase their miscarriage kit. It will provide you with almost everything you need to catch your baby. If the kit will not arrive in time or you are worried the kit may not arrive in time, you can purchase these items at a local store.

- Colander
- Small jars like mason jars or other glass jars with lids
- Saline — contact lens solution works
- Large plastic bag to place the colander in after use
- Rubber gloves
- Squirt bottle or plastic cup for rinsing clots/blood off contents
- Menstrual Pads
- Incontinence pads to protect mattresses or couches/chairs from heavy bleeding
- Brown paper bag

Every time you go to the restroom, take the colander with you and place it in the toilet before sitting down to pee or pass clots. The colander will capture the clots. After cleaning yourself, use the squirt bottle to rinse the clots or blood off tissues. If you see gray, white, tan, or other colors, this is most likely the baby, sac, placenta, and/or umbilical cord. If you don't have a squirt bottle, use a cup to rinse the clots with water. The rubber gloves will help you sift through the clots and blood. This may be very difficult for you or even embarrassing. If you need help, ask your husband or a trusted friend.

Place the rinsed content in one of the jars and seal it. If you have saline, you may fill the jar with saline. This may provide an opportunity for you to see your tiny baby. Place the jar in a brown paper bag or similar and set in the refrigerator. Then contact your local Catholic funeral or cemetery services for burial. The following chapter explains the options for your baby's body in more detail.

Never go through a miscarriage alone. Your bleeding can quickly turn to hemorrhaging, and you can pass out. Have someone with you while you are actively cramping and bleeding heavily. If you are feeling faint or dizzy, call 911.

And the dust returns to the earth as it was, and the spirit returns to God who gave it. – ECCLESIASTES 12:7

CHAPTER FIVE: OPTIONS FOR YOUR BABY'S BODY

Baptism

If your baby is born alive, baptism is a necessity. If you see a heartbeat, or movement of any kind, or your baby attempts to breathe, have him or her baptized. This may require preparing ahead to have a priest with you. If your baby is not breathing, or if it is not clear if the baby is alive, the baby should be baptized *sub conditione,* in case the baby is still alive. The Catholic Church's position is that babies (including those miscarried), in danger of death, can be baptized.

If a priest cannot be present, you or your husband can perform an emergency baptism, but really anyone can perform an emergency baptism. All you need is some water (it does not have to be holy water), and utilize the correct formula. "[Baby's name], I baptize you in the name of the Father, and of the Son, and of the Holy Spirit," while simultaneously pouring water over the baby's head or immersing them in water three times (Father, Son, Holy Spirit). At the very minimum, one witness should be present to prove baptism.

The church has always taught that baptism is necessary for salvation. If we believe that unbaptized babies are given grace and receive salvation regardless of baptism, this goes against Church teaching. This belief is called Original Grace and is a heresy. What would be the need for baptism if Original Grace existed? The Lord himself affirms that baptism is necessary for salvation in John 3:5.

The information here is not to cause pain. This is truly a difficult part of church teaching to accept and is an area the Church would do good to come out an explain. While we ultimately do not know what happens when unbaptized babies die; we should have hope.

> *"Let the children come to me, do not hinder them; for to such belongs the Kingdom of God." – Mk 10:14*

The question remains — If baptism washes away original sin, and my baby wasn't baptized, what hope then is there for my baby? See Chapter Eight: Where is My Baby? The Catholic Health Association of the United States has a helpful document for hospital chaplains called, "Baptizing" Deceased Infants[9].

Bonding

Even with the tiniest of babies, you have options for bonding. The options available to you will depend on the type of delivery. The options below are noted with **S** for Surgical Birth which includes D&C/D&E, **M** for Medical Management, and **E** for Expectant Management to help you understand and possibly plan for your delivery based on what is important to you.

- Cut the baby's cord. (M, E)
- Cord or placenta print*. (M, E)
- Submerge your baby in water or saline to hold/photograph/preserve details**. (M, E)

- Hold your baby (even if the baby only fits in the palm of your hand). (M, E)
- Play music. Use music to imprint your brain and help you bond with your baby. Many women choose one song that is very meaningful to them. (S, M, E)
- Use essential oils. Create a specific blend of oils to diffuse in your room as you hold and bond with your baby. (S, M, E)
- Take pictures with and of your baby. You may never want to look at them again, but knowing you have them available to view any time you want can be very comforting. (M, E)
- Have hand/footprints or hand/foot molds done by the hospital staff. Even tiny babies as early as 14 weeks can have their handprints and footprints taken by a skilled staff member, or you may try this at home. (M, E, S (for later gestations))
- Bathe, diaper, and/or dress your baby. There are tiny wraps, diapers, and hats made for babies as small as 12 weeks gestation. (M, E)
- Wrap the baby (special blanket or outfit). (M, E)
- Have your baby baptized (if born alive). (M, E)
- Have your baby blessed. (S, M, E)
- Name your baby. (S, M, E)

*To create a cord or placenta print, all that is needed is a piece of paper, preferably white paper, and simply press the cord and/or placenta to the paper to create a "print." If there is no longer blood on the cord/placenta, or you do not want the print to be made from blood, you will need some paint.

** Submerging your baby in water inside a clear bowl/tank will delay the decomposition process and allow you to see the tiniest of features on your baby. Some have been able to preserve/bond with their babies for several days before burial. Saline or salt water significantly helps with babies who have passed from hydrops (swelling/edema) and will reduce swelling, revealing even more of your baby's features.

Final Disposition for the Physical Form of Your Baby's Body

It is important to understand that a human being, formed at the moment of fertilization, should be respected and treated with dignity upon death. *"The corpses of human embryos and fetuses, whether they have been deliberately aborted or not, must be respected just as the remains of other human beings"* – Donum Vitae[10]. Therefore, you have the right to choose the final arrangements of your baby's body regardless of gestational age or place of birth. Your baby is a part of the community of faith and is important enough to warrant dignity and respect, even in death.

Your medical provider may only offer you secular options, and not all are in line with Catholic teaching. It is your right to demand a disposition in line with your religious practices. For example: in Colorado, your doctor may not make it known that you have a right to your baby's body, but by law, you do, so long as the mother asks. Without the doctor telling you this though, you might not know to ask.

Several options are available, with the most common options being burial (communal or separate), cremation (hospital incineration or private), and hospital disposition. Hospital disposition and/or cremation likely means your baby will be incinerated with other "medical waste." The human person should never be treated as medical waste. Burial and cremation are discussed below.

If your hospital is unsure how to proceed, provide them with the Guidance on Disposition of Fetal Remains[11], which addresses remains for miscarriage and stillbirth. Unfortunately, you might need to educate your priest during this difficult time. Many are not well-versed in pregnancy loss despite how common this is. Please donate this book to your parish priest and/or parish library.

Can I have a Funeral Mass?

If your baby was able to be baptized, you should have a funeral Mass. The current Catechism of the Catholic Church and current Code of Canon Law allows for a funeral Mass for unbaptized infants even though baptism is necessary for salvation (CCC 1257 and Jn 3:3-5). God, however, is not bound by the sacraments. This is why the unbaptized, through no fault of their own, may achieve salvation. Babies specifically are entrusted to the mercy of God.

According to the Order of Christian Funerals #237, "Funeral rites may be celebrated for children whose parents intended them to be baptized but who died before baptism. In these celebrations the Christian community entrusts the child to God's all-embracing love and finds strength in this love and in Jesus' affirmation that the kingdom of God belongs to little children (see Mt 19:14)."

Code of Canon Law, Canon 1183 states, "The local ordinary can permit children whom the parents intended to baptize but who died before baptism to be given ecclesiastical funerals." A funeral Mass is an act of worship, not a celebration of life. This liturgy is used to pray for the deceased and entrust their soul to God's mercy in the hopes they bypass purgatory, or that their suffering in purgatory is short.

Naming and Commendation Ceremony/Memorial Service

If your baby was unable to be baptized, you can still ask for a funeral Mass. If you don't feel that's appropriate, you can request a Naming and Commendation ceremony. This is also in the Order of Christian Funerals. It is similar to a memorial service and can be very healing. It is a celebration of life for your child who lived, even if it was for a short time.

Some families send out invitations or call/text friends and family to ask them to come to the ceremony. The ceremony might look similar to a wake, with flowers and a table displaying the baby's name, pictures from pregnancy, ultrasound pictures, and other items they might have to remember their baby. A sign-in book can also be purchased, and this could be added to a memory box.

Prayers or thoughts/poems could be read by those who attend, and there may be an opportunity for people to come forward and speak. This ceremony isn't necessary, so there is no obligation to have one, but many find it very healing, especially if a funeral Mass didn't feel appropriate or the request was denied by the local ordinariate.

Burial

Many Catholic cemeteries and/or dioceses have a burial location for miscarried or stillborn babies, or you may purchase a plot. Communal burial plots are also available. This is where many babies are buried in the same plot. There is usually a Rite of Committal that family and friends may attend. One downside to communal burial plots is that there may or may not be an option to have a grave marker with your baby's name at the location. Contact your parish priest or archdiocese to inquire about burial locations. Some cemeteries may also allow your baby to be buried with another family member.

Your baby is part of the community of faith and should be buried. In each case, it is the responsibility of the parents to make the arrangements. Calling a local funeral home will help get you started, but sometimes healthcare professionals and/or hospitals may assist with this process.

Getting recommendations from friends and family can be helpful when making this decision. Sometimes it is too difficult for you and your husband to make these arrangements. If it feels difficult, ask a family member or friend to make the calls for you. There are also perinatal loss specialists and bereavement doulas in many areas who can assist you.

Cremation

This option is available for Catholics, although it is not the preferred option. Ideally, the cremation should take place after the funeral Mass. Please talk with your parish priest or archdiocese to ensure the proper format occurs. If you are reading this and your baby was cremated prior to the funeral Mass, the diocesan bishop may allow for the cremains at the funeral Mass. The Rite of Committal will then take place as your baby's remains are placed in the mausoleum or columbarium.

The cremated remains of a body should be treated with the same respect given to the human body from which they come. This includes the use of a worthy vessel to contain the ashes, the manner in which they are carried, the care and attention to appropriate placement and transport, and the final disposition. The cremated remains should be buried in a grave or entombed in a mausoleum or columbarium. The practice of scattering cremated remains on the sea, from the air, or on the ground, or keeping cremated remains in your home (only in grave circumstances with permission from the bishop). or the home of a relative or friend of the deceased is not the reverent disposition that the Church requires. (OCF no. 417)

As the parents, you are responsible for choosing a funeral home for the cremation of your baby's remains, although your archdiocese may have resources for you. If your baby was not able to be baptized, the remains should still be treated with honor and respect even though a funeral Mass cannot be offered. It is very important that you understand that your baby's ashes must be buried or placed in a niche, preferably in a Catholic cemetery, but any cemetery or a sacred place will suffice. Ashes are not to be worn, turned into jewelry or other fashionable items.

Note:
Due to the small size of some babies, there may not be enough ashes to return to you. Sometimes, crematories will let you burn items with your baby, such as letters or clothing, in order to create more ashes, but this policy will vary with each crematory.

Hospital Disposition

It is not recommended that this option is chosen. With this option, the baby's remains are rarely returned to you. If cost is the reason, please reach out to your parish and/or archdiocese and ask them for help in providing the respect and dignity your baby deserves. Hospital disposition usually means your baby will be incinerated in an approved medical incinerator. Your baby may or may not be incinerated with hospital/medical waste. Some hospitals incinerate babies separated from medical waste, but not all do this.

If you are offered to have your baby's remains returned, your baby's ashes would need to be buried or placed in a niche, as stated above. Some hospitals release the ashes of babies in an area on hospital grounds, usually at a memorial site, that families can visit. This is not in line with Catholic teaching and should not occur. You have to be extremely diligent to ensure your baby's ashes are not scattered if you choose this option.

Note:
Many funeral homes and crematories offer their services at reduced rates, and some even provide them for free. Please check with your local funeral homes and crematories to see if this is offered there. Most will tell you upfront as a courtesy. In some areas, the coffin is also free, although it is a basic coffin. Urns are usually not free.

I Flushed...Now What?

This is a very common concern or one you may not have even considered. Flushing can come with extreme feelings of guilt and shame. It's part of this experience that many women do not talk about, but even if you flushed, that does not mean you didn't love your baby.

Many women flush out of routine or out of fear. Automatic toilets can flush too quickly for you to retrieve the tissues. Some women don't even consider it, while other women had no means to catch the tissues, but there are still options for you. Talk with your priest about this. He may have some other offerings for you, and at the very least, can pray for you and your baby.

If you are experiencing an inevitable miscarriage, it may be worth carrying around a small container or bag in case it happens outside your home. You could also carry around some gloves in case the tissues fall into the toilet, and you want to reach in and retrieve them. You could then close your gloved hand and pull off the glove so that it's inside out and the remains are inside the glove.

You could bring the remains home to store in the fridge until you reach a funeral home. Some women have taken remains to the hospital emergency room, but they would be processed according to hospital disposal procedures. Testing is not impossible at this point, but many doctors will say it's not an option, especially if this is your first miscarriage; however, you can pay for testing. If you want to test your baby's remains for sex or genetic abnormalities, demand it. There is a more detailed list of things to have on hand for miscarriage in Chapter Four.

The guilt and shame of flushing, whether you had an option or not, can be difficult to process. One option that might be helpful for you is to say goodbye "officially." A water ceremony for miscarriage can help you say goodbye and bring peace in this situation, but the best way to say goodbye is to celebrate a Mass for the child.

To have a water ceremony, find a body of water such as a river, pond, lake, etc. Some couples also choose to have family and/or friends with them, but this could be done alone or as a couple. Dress up and meet at the body of water. You could say a prayer, ask God for forgiveness if it feels right to you, and/or tell your baby how much you love him or her and will miss them.

Here is a sample prayer:

"Little one [or insert baby's name], you have been received by the water, 'For as the rain and the snow come down from heaven and do not return there without watering the earth and making it bear and sprout, and furnishing seed to the sower and bread to the eater;' you have returned to the earth and your spirit returns to God who gave it." Adapted from Isaiah 55:10 and Ecclesiastes 12:7

> *The dignity of the human person is rooted in his creation in the image and likeness of God.–*
> *CCC 1700*

For I have no pleasure in the death of anyone, declares the Lord God; so turn, and live. – EZEKIEL 18:32

CHAPTER SIX: AFTER THE MISCARRIAGE

Caring for Your Postpartum Body

Even though you didn't deliver a full-term baby, the physical and emotional states are very much like that of a postpartum mother. You need to care for your body in the same way. Below is a list of things to help you care for your postpartum body.

- Take naps and try to get plenty of rest.
- Limit visitors unless visits are emotionally healing for you.
- Your bleeding will get lighter as the days progress, but you may bleed for up to six weeks.
- Your bleeding may increase with too much activity. If you notice bright red blood or blood after you stopped bleeding, you may have engaged in too much physical activity. The placenta leaves a wound in your womb that needs time to heal. Exercise is very helpful but start slow and easy.
- Nothing should be placed in your vagina for several weeks (consult your obstetrician). This includes sexual intercourse, tampons, menstrual cups, and devices that strengthen the perineal muscles or fingers.

Introducing anything into the vagina increases your risk of infection.

- Lifting should be restricted to items less than 15 pounds.
- Household chores should be put on hold or completed by someone else for the first few weeks while your body heals.
- Eat healthy foods. This may be difficult as you may not feel hungry.
- Drink plenty of fluids (at least six to eight glasses of water per day)
- Change your pads every two to three hours. This will help reduce the risk of infection.
- If you received a peri bottle, use this every time you urinate for the first week. (Most women with first-trimester miscarriages will not receive this).
- If you have vaginal pain in your perineum, you can soak in a small amount of water in the bathtub. Adding a little Epsom Salt can also help. A hemorrhoid pillow is helpful and can be found at most drug stores.
- Increase your fiber intake and take a stool softener and/or laxative to help with any constipation. Short walks every day will also help move your bowels and reduce constipation.
- Urinate every three to five hours to reduce the risk of contracting a bladder infection.
- Do not be afraid to take pain medications like acetaminophen (Tylenol®) or ibuprofen (Advil®) if you need to. Do not feel like you "deserve" pain or need to suffer more than you already have. Follow the package labeling recommendations on dose and frequency.
- Do not drive if you are taking narcotics for pain.

- Avoid smoking, illegal drugs, marijuana, and alcohol, and limit caffeine consumption.
- Pray — there are many prayers you might find helpful throughout this book.

What You Might Feel

Everyone feels differently about miscarriage and pregnancy loss. There is no right or wrong way to grieve, and there is no timeline for the grief you may experience. It is important, if you are grieving, to spend time mourning this loss.

You may be surprised by how you feel, especially if you felt that miscarriage was not a big deal prior to your own personal loss. You may show very little grief in the early days but experience intense grief months or even years later. This is normal. This just means everyone grieves differently. Some may never grieve the loss of their baby. This is okay too. It is important not to feel bad if your feelings are not as intense as someone else's.

Your husband may react differently than you would expect, which can cause friction between the two of you. Try to keep in mind that everyone grieves differently. Even if he isn't mourning the loss, he may still be upset.

Another common reaction is feeling like you are still pregnant. It takes time for the body to return to the pre-pregnant state, and sometimes you may forget that you miscarried. You may find yourself still rubbing your belly, avoiding things that would have been harmful during pregnancy, and possibly yearning to hold a baby. This is also normal, although it can be emotionally painful. Some women purchase a teddy bear to carry, which helps with the yearning to hold a baby.

You may be worried that you will never feel normal or like yourself again. You may wonder when the sadness will go away. There is no way to tell how long you will feel sad.

Emotional Expression

You may feel emotional, weepy, confused, tearful, anxious, easily upset, overly sensitive, irritable, angry, nervous, very tired, indifferent, or a vast array of other emotions. All of these feelings are normal. It takes time to heal both emotionally and physically following the loss of a baby. Be gentle with yourself as you navigate through these feelings.

You may be wondering why God did this to you, why He took your baby, and why you are being punished. You may feel you did not pray enough or weren't a good enough Catholic, or you may begin to doubt your faith. God is calling you to come to Him. He did not "take" your baby (i.e., "God needed another angel"). He is not punishing you.

"And his disciples ask him, 'Rabbi, who sinned, this man or his parents, that he was born blind?' Jesus answered, 'It was not that this man sinned, or his parents, but that the works of God might be made manifest in him.'" – John 9:2-3

God allows suffering. Through suffering, grace happens. St. Bernadette may be the saint you call upon for intercession during this time. Although many saints suffered, Our Lady of Lourdes once said to St. Bernadette, *"I do not promise to make you happy in this life, but in the next."*

Grief can be very isolating, and it tends to come in waves. What you need today, you may not need tomorrow, but then need again a day or two later. Mothers often find comfort in a place where they can openly express their grief and find acknowledgment for their pain. Cry with someone. Connect with someone who seems to understand. They may or may not have experienced a pregnancy loss, but it can be very comforting if they offer a shoulder.

Physical Reactions and Experiences

You can have physical reactions to grief, such as heart palpitations, insomnia, headaches, loss of appetite, stomachaches, inability to concentrate, and/or withdrawal from friends and family or events. Some women have a physical aching in their arms due to the desire to hold and nurture their babies. Other women have phantom kicks. All of these are normal but can be distressing.

Many women report having scary dreams or nightmares. This can occur both before the loss and after. Some women who had dreams of their baby dying prior to the miscarriage look back and believe this dream was preparing them.

You may bleed or spot for a few weeks, experience cramping, your period may not resume for several weeks, and you may produce milk or experience breast engorgement. You also have pregnancy hormones in your body that could take months to get out of your system.

Due to your body changing from a pregnant state to a non-pregnant state, you may not want to have sex. Talk with your husband about this. It's just like after you have a baby. Your vagina may hurt, you may be bleeding, and you may feel this could lead you down the road to another failed pregnancy.

Your hormones will be off-kilter because they are returning to a pre-pregnancy state. This is all normal. If it's debilitating for you, contact your doctor or OB/GYN. It shouldn't be years before you feel like having sex again, but a few months isn't atypical.

Grief and Postpartum Depression

There are hormone changes in a woman's body that can affect her emotions. If you are struggling to complete daily tasks such as showering, changing your clothes, getting out of bed, etc., it's time to speak with a therapist. The same warnings for postpartum depression apply after a pregnancy loss. In fact, 12% of women will experience depression, and 20% will experience a combination of depression and grief. Grief is a normal part of the bereavement process and is separate from depression. You may experience all the stages of grief — denial, anger, guilt, depression, and acceptance — or just a few.

Also, understand that if you are given an antidepressant to treat grief, this is not the most effective treatment method. An antidepressant can cause suicidal ideation or exacerbate thoughts of suicide. However, complicated grief can occur, and an antidepressant may be appropriate. Antidepressants should only be prescribed by your doctor in conjunction with recommendations by your therapist.

If you're feeling sad and weepy for longer than two weeks, feel no desire to live, have had thoughts of suicide, or have planned your suicide, seek treatment immediately. If you have a plan for suicide, you need to immediately check into an emergency department. Text HOME to

741741 or call 1-800-273-8255. Please be prepared for law enforcement and/or an ambulance to arrive.

Grief may last a long time, but you shouldn't be weepy every hour of every day. The weepiness should gradually improve. Even if you spent five minutes less weeping today versus yesterday, that's an improvement. You will feel better. If you don't feel your enthusiasm for life returning, you should seek help from a therapist specializing in pregnancy loss and/or postpartum mood disorders.

Grief is painful, but it is possible to move forward when one is ready. Some women feel they have moved through their grief after only a week, and other women are still grieving decades after their loss. Grief has no timeline.

At some point, you will most likely feel some sense of normalcy again. Some women describe feeling guilty when they start to feel normal or like themselves as if that means they have somehow betrayed their baby. Remember that moving forward and rejoining the living doesn't mean you have forgotten your loss and its impact. You will have good days and bad days, and then one day, you might realize that you are having more good days than bad. Only then will you know you are adapting to your new normal.

For I know well the plans I have in mind for you, says the Lord, plans for your welfare, not for woe! Plans to give you a future full of hope. – JEREMIAH 29:11

CHAPTER SEVEN: CAUSES

The Search for a Cause

Women often search for a reason for their baby's death. This is very natural. A cause isn't always found, and sometimes it's just that our baby was not going to take a breath of air on this earth. God did not cause this. God allowed this, and he does not take joy in it. We may need to reframe our minds.

> *"Sometimes we have "inside only" babies." – Dede Chism at Bella Health + Wellness in Englewood, CO*

You have some options that are licit and in line with Church teaching. For older babies, you have the option of having an autopsy. For babies born in the first trimester, placenta testing or products of conception testing is an option, although you may have to inquire heavily to receive this.

You will have little chance of finding a cause if you do not request testing. Still, for some women, the pain of what an autopsy entails or the kind of testing available may stop them from requesting the tests. You must do what you are comfortable with. If you think you will regret not testing, it's worth asking your doctor or facility about available options. There are always options, and, unfortunately, some providers and facilities will use the excuse that testing isn't available due to their own biases. There ARE tests, even for the tiniest of babies, if you want to know.

Many women will blame themselves and feel they did something to cause the miscarriage. In most cases, you did nothing to cause a miscarriage, nor are you cursed in some way. Below is a list of things that **do not cause miscarriage**:

- Physical exercise/exertion
- Sports activities
- Work
- Anxiety
- Sexual intercourse
- Travel
- Lifting
- Occasional use of alcohol or most over-the-counter medications
- Exhaust fumes
- Sin

If I Didn't Cause This, Why Did My Baby Die?

Studies show that a cause or reason for the baby's death is found less than 50% of the time; however, if most doctors don't offer the testing, we really won't have good answers. In addition, autopsies occur in less than 13% of all stillbirths. An autopsy to determine how a person died is ethical and allowed by the Catholic Church[12], but the utmost respect for the human remains of the person must be observed.

As shared above, some families find comfort in not knowing, and others struggle when they don't have a reason. Give yourself time to discern this. There is no rush to come to a decision right away.

Below are some listed causes of miscarriage.

The number one cited reason for miscarriage before 12 weeks gestation is a **genetic abnormality** with the baby. While the cells are dividing, sometimes DNA translocates or causes a genetic error, which results in poor development or fatal conditions. There is no licit way to prevent a genetic error. Reproductive technologies have been used to select genetically perfect children; however, this is done through selective abortion, and these technologies go against Catholic teaching and the Will of God.

Failure of the egg to properly implant into the lining of the uterus is a common cause.

Low progesterone is another common reason for miscarriage. This can be diagnosed during pregnancy, and supplementation of this important hormone can be started. While some studies do not show that supplementation with progesterone prevents miscarriage, progesterone does support a pregnancy. Progesterone thickens the lining of the uterus, which is where the very early and developing baby implants and receives its nutrients in order to grow. With low levels of progesterone, a baby may not have the nutrients needed until the placenta grows and takes over this critical function. A NaProTECHNOLOGY© practitioner can help you test, balance, and manage your progesterone levels.

Uterine anomalies are another cause of miscarriage. Some women have scar tissue in the uterus from a previous abortion or D&C/D&E procedure, endometriosis, uterine infection, C-section or other uterine surgery, fibroids, polyps or other uterine growths, septate uterus, or congenital uterine abnormalities developed in your mother's womb may also cause uterine anomalies.

Incompetent cervix is another cause of miscarriage. This is where the cervix, which is the opening of your uterus, cannot hold the baby's weight and dilates (opens) and effaces (softens, shortens, and becomes thinner) too early. The baby would then be born (alive or deceased), but if this occurs before 22 weeks, the baby would be too premature for medical providers to utilize any life-saving measures.

An incompetent cervix is most often diagnosed in the second trimester, although some women have experienced an incompetent cervix earlier. Sometimes, in a threatened miscarriage, this issue can be diagnosed and treated, but it is often not treated until a subsequent pregnancy. Treatment includes surgically closing the cervix with a purse-string type stitch known as cervical cerclage. These stitches are removed once you reach full term. A transabdominal cerclage may be needed for recurring incompetent cervix or women with short cervices.

Blood disorders are also a reason for miscarriage. Blood disorders such as MTHFR or other disorders that affect clotting are common, but women are often not tested for these clotting and antigen disorders until they have had several early miscarriages. Some of these disorders can be treated with medications in subsequent pregnancies.

Very rarely, **infections** can cause miscarriage. Infections such as Rubella, Human Parvovirus B19 (Fifth's Disease),

Varicella (Chicken Pox), or untreated bacterial infections have caused miscarriage.

Will This Happen Again?

If a treatable condition is found and treated for future pregnancies, the risk of miscarriage decreases; however, there is always a risk. Your chances of having a successful pregnancy following a miscarriage are about the same as if you had never had a miscarriage in the past. You may need additional monitoring in future pregnancies, but many women go on to have healthy babies.

Now faith is the assurance of things hoped for, the conviction of things not seen. – HEBREWS 11:1

CHAPTER EIGHT: WHERE IS MY BABY?

Is My Baby an Angel?

No, your baby cannot be an angel. Angels are pure and bodiless spirits created at the beginning of time. They are purely spiritual in nature. Their "nature" is a bodiless one. There is nothing physical about them. So, God does not have another "angel in heaven." Humans are entirely separate creatures from angels and can procreate. Angels cannot. Your baby had a body and a soul, created in His image and likeness. While humans, including babies, cannot become angels, they can become saints.

Babies baptized at birth would not experience purgatory and, thus, would be received into Heaven as a saint. There are many kinds of saints. Our babies do not need to be officially recognized by the church to be saints. Saints aren't just the incorruptible, like Padre Pio. They are part of the community of saints, which we hear about at every Mass. If your baby was baptized, he or she is sinless and, therefore, has no need for purification in purgatory. Your baby can be a powerful intercessor for you.

If your baby was unable to be baptized, the current Catechism of the Catholic Church tells us this:

> *"As regards children who have died without Baptism, the Church can only entrust them to the mercy of God, as she does in her funeral rites for them. Indeed, the great mercy of God who desires that all men should be saved, and Jesus' tenderness toward children which caused him to say: "Let the children come to me, do not hinder them," allow us to hope that there is a way of salvation for children who have died without Baptism. All the more urgent is the Church's call not to prevent little children from coming to Christ through the gift of holy Baptism."* CCC1261

The above passage is cause for hope as is this: *"Our conclusion is that the many factors that we have considered above give serious theological and liturgical grounds for hope that unbaptized infants who die will be saved and enjoy the Beatific Vision. We emphasize that these are reasons for prayerful hope, rather than grounds for sure knowledge."* – The Hope of Salvation for Infants Who Die Without Baptism [102]

Is My Baby in Limbo?

The very thought of Limbo conjures up images of souls suspended in a perpetual state of abandonment and no parent wants to imagine their tiny baby as abandoned by God. According to current Church teaching though, Limbo is still a possibility for unbaptized babies. The vast majority of people do not understand Limbo so it will be explained here.

While the term Limbo or Limbus in Latin means "edge," souls in this state are not abandoned nor in a perpetual state of suspension. The name Limbo was probably chosen on account of St. Augustine's (354-430AD) pessimistic view that infants who die unbaptized are consigned to the fringes of Hell and suffer the mildest of punishments. He had to hold strong against Pelagianism.

The Limbo of the Infants is not the same as the Limbo of the Patriarchs, which many Catholics are familiar with because it is attested to in the Creed. When the Creed says that Jesus descended into hell, it refers to his descent to the Limbo of the Patriarchs, where the 'just' from the Old Testament were detained. The 'just' were those who died in a state of grace and were assured of their salvation but before Christ's work of redemption, e.g., St. Joseph, Abraham, and King David. After his death, Jesus announced to these souls the long-awaited redemption. After the Lord's Resurrection and Ascension, they too, entered heaven. The Limbo of the Patriarchs, therefore, was only a temporary state and is empty.

What then, is the Limbo of the Infants? Limbo of the Infants is a place of natural happiness wherein souls glorify God. Why might unbaptized babies be in Limbo? Because baptism is necessary for salvation. Even babies in the womb are subject to the effects of Original Sin because the only human preserved from Original Sin is Mary; which is why we say "Queen conceived without Original Sin." Is God so cruel He would damn even an innocent child that dies in the womb?

Man is made in God's image and likeness, this includes babies, and all of human creation is ordered to know and love God. God cannot create a rational creature without ordering the creature to Himself. Rational creatures seek explanations, and the ultimate explanation is God because He orders all things. On a purely natural level, the purpose of our existence is to seek, know, and love God.

> *"For what can be known about God is plain to them, because God has shown it to them. Ever since the creation of the world his invisible nature, namely, his eternal power and deity, has been clearly perceived in the things which have been made."* – Romans 1:19-20.

Given that this is the purpose of human nature, it must be attainable: if the purpose - the natural end - of human nature is unattainable, then that nature becomes purposeless and meaningless. God cannot create a purposeless nature. He inscribes in our hearts the knowledge of Natural Law, to differentiate between good and evil. Part of that law is to love our neighbor.

The Decalogue — the Ten Commandments — are a minimal statement of the Natural Law, that law of God written into human nature, which is written upon the heart. Seven of those ten commandments pertain to our neighbor - to do no evil to our neighbor. The Golden Rule - do unto others as you would have them do unto you (Mt 7:12) - is not only an ordinance of grace, it is an ordinance of nature.

The souls in Limbo are in a state of loving communion with each other, contemplating the God of creation known through His creatures. These souls are in a natural state of happiness, experiencing no pain. There is no punishment, nor are they suffering a purification. They feel no sorrow nor any sense of loss. Limbo then, is not only not a place of "abandoned souls," it is not a place of isolated contemplation.

This is how God created these souls to love Him. The souls in Limbo cannot possibly know of the supernatural destiny of heaven precisely because it is supernatural. As St. Paul teaches: *"What eye has not seen, nor ear heard, nor the heart of man conceived, what God has prepared for those who love him."* – 1 Corinthians 2:9

The children in Limbo then, are fulfilling the purpose of their existence. This is a part of God's design and a great mystery: *"O the depth of the riches and wisdom and knowledge of God! How unsearchable are his judgments and how inscrutable his ways! "For who has known the mind of the Lord, or who has been his counselor?"... For from him and through him and to him are all things. To him be glory forever. Amen."* – Romans 11:33-36. Limbo isn't a place we should fear or worry for our children who may be there.

For some readers, this may be the first time hearing about Limbo or you've heard but believe this is very old and no longer true. The earliest documentation on Limbo is from St. Gregory Nazianzus, Oration 40, (329-390AD). It is also found in the Catechism of the Council of Trent (1545-1563 AD), the Catechism of Pope Saint Pius X (1908), and the Baltimore Catechism. The debates about the Limbo of the Infants likely arose as a response to questions about where unbaptized children go when they die on account of Original Sin. Clearly, unbaptized babies don't go to hell as they cannot commit mortal sin, yet without baptism, how can they go directly to Heaven?

Pope Saint John Paul II had the International Theological Commission study what happens to unbaptized infants who die. In 2007, Pope Benedict XIV approved a document for publication entitled, *The Hope of Salvation for Infants Who Die Without Baptism*[13].

"This theory, elaborated by theologians beginning in the Middle Ages, never entered into the dogmatic definitions of the Magisterium, even if that same Magisterium did at times mention the theory in its ordinary teaching up until the Second Vatican Council.

> *It remains therefore a possible theological hypothesis. However, in the Catechism of the Catholic Church (1992), the theory of limbo is not mentioned. Rather, the Catechism teaches that infants who die without baptism are entrusted by the Church to the mercy of God, as is shown in the specific funeral rite for such children." – excerpt from The Hope of Salvation for Infants Who Die Without Baptism.*

In conclusion, Limbo was the common Catholic teaching until the mid-20th century, it is not dogma, and other opinions do exist.

> *"God has bound salvation to the sacrament of Baptism, but he himself is not bound by his sacraments."* – CCC1257

Therefore, God may save anyone He chooses and in theory, you are free to believe your baby is in Heaven. We will not fully understand this as we can only see through our bodily eyes and the lens of our humanity. In the end, all will be revealed and we will understand. Until then, we can still pray for our babies. In fact, you should pray for them.

God will use your prayers as He sees fit. Give your baby a proper name and while you go through your grieving process, talk with your baby; in the same way you talk with God or another loved one who is deceased. Visit your baby's grave, which can be very comforting, especially in the early months of loss and on anniversaries. Your goal is to know God, love Him, and serve Him so you can be happy with Him forever in Heaven. You will want for nothing when you are in eternal happiness with God.

Trust in the LORD with all your heart, and do not rely on your own insight. – PROVERBS 3:5

CHAPTER NINE: SUFFERING

This book aims to provide immediate guidance on what to do when you learn you are having a miscarriage or a miscarriage is impending. However, it would not be complete without some understanding of suffering and resources to help with your suffering. A summary is listed here, and more Catholic books on suffering are listed in the resources section of this book.

God loves you, even in suffering. In fact, he loves you so much that God himself entered into your suffering through Jesus. Jesus suffered and died on the cross… for you. However, it is very difficult to feel God's love in these moments, but it is there, and God is waiting for you to offer this suffering to Him. It's also okay to ask God why. It's okay to be sad, but don't let go of God. God is not punishing you for not praying enough or not giving enough. This is a trial that must be endured.

We are not made for this world, and many times it is forgotten that this world is full of pain and suffering. We are not meant to avoid trials on this earth. Our trials are for a purpose, even though they hurt. St. James tries to help us understand suffering a bit more when he says, *"Count it all joy, my brethren, when you meet various trials, for you know that the testing of your faith produces steadfastness."* – James 1:2

St. James is explaining that our suffering produces something. That 'something' should be perseverance. It should create a stronger faith when you do not allow your trials to crush your faith. This means we must allow Christ into our suffering in hopes of developing what is called resilient faith. Pope John Paul II wrote an Apostolic Letter on suffering called *Salvifici Doloris*.

> *"In order to discover the profound meaning of suffering, following the revealed word of God, we must open ourselves wide to the human subject in his manifold potentiality. We must above all accept the light of Revelation not only insofar as it expresses the transcendent order of justice but also insofar as it illuminates this order with Love, as the definitive source of everything that exists. Love is: also the fullest source of the answer to the question of the meaning of suffering. This answer has been given by God to man in the Cross of Jesus Christ."* – Salvifici Doloris [13]

You aren't suffering because God doesn't love you. You are not cursed. You did not fail to pray hard enough. Tell God how much you are suffering. Tell Him everything! This life comes with suffering because of our fallen nature, but God wants us to be happy with Him in heaven. When that day comes, there will be no suffering.

No one rejoices in your suffering. In fact, many are suffering alongside you. Your suffering gives others the opportunity for charity and compassion. Through suffering comes great charity and the growth of virtue in others — Masses said for you, meals brought to you, prayers offered for you, housework done for you, and more. This suffering is a participation in God's work on the world.

"It is not by sidestepping or fleeing from suffering that we are healed but rather by our capacity for accepting it, maturing through it and finding meaning through union with Christ, who suffered with infinite love." – Pope Benedict XVI

Until then, we must use our suffering for the good of others by allowing others to serve us and offer up our suffering to save souls. This is not the Catholic way of saying, "Get over it." Offering it up is a deliberate and thoughtful process.

What Does it Mean to Offer It Up?

Offering up your suffering is called redemptive suffering. When we do this, we offer up our suffering as a sacrifice to God for the good of others. This is how you can unite yourself to Christ.

Suffering doesn't feel good, but when we know that our suffering can be for someone else's good and remind ourselves of that often, sometimes it makes it a bit easier to endure the suffering. Your suffering may help purify you if you allow it. It may humble you if you are a person who does not like to rely on others, but in this suffering, you need to allow others to help you.

How do I Offer It Up?

Offering it up is as simple as saying, "Lord, I am hurting, and I offer this to you for the sake of [insert name]." There may be moments where you feel you are constantly offering suffering. If it's difficult for you to allow someone to help you or do something for you, say, "Lord, I offer this sacrifice to you for [insert name]." If your day is going to be particularly hard, begin with the morning offering:

"O Jesus, through the Immaculate Heart of Mary, I offer you my prayers, works, joys, and sufferings of this day for all the intentions of your Sacred Heart in union with the Holy Sacrifice of the Mass throughout the world, for the salvation of souls, the reparation of sins, the reunion of all Christians, and in particular for the intentions of the Holy Father this month. Amen." (Written in 1844 AD by Fr. François-Xavier Gautrelet; found in Catholic Household Blessings and Prayers, pg. 48)

Look for opportunities throughout your day to offer it up. Anything from complaints to pains and annoyances can be offered quickly and easily to God. The offerings do not have to be big things or serious problems, anything that disturbs your peace or prevents you from gaining peace is an offering.

"I couldn't pray at all, at least, not for myself. I found that if I had other people's intentions and prayer requests, prayer was at least bearable, and I prayed more." – Jessica

Ask your friends and family if they could use prayers for themselves or a deceased loved one. Create a list of all those prayers your family and friends need and offer them up. Another helpful prayer for offering up your suffering comes from Colossians.

"I now rejoice in my sufferings for you, and fill up in my flesh what is lacking in the afflictions of Christ,

for the sake of His body, which is the Church." – Colossians 1:24

Saints Who Suffered

You are not alone in your suffering. Many have suffered before you. Our Blessed Mother understands suffering better than anyone. She accepted suffering when she said "Yes" to God. Simeon, at the Presentation in the Temple, said to Mary, *"Behold, this child is set for the fall and rising of many in Israel, and for a sign that is spoken against (and a sword will pierce through your own soul also), that the thoughts out of many hearts may be revealed."* – Luke 2:33-35

Mary set Jesus' mission in motion at the Wedding at Cana when the wedding couple ran out of wine. When Mary pointed out that the wine failed, Jesus replies, *"O Woman, what have you to do with me? My hour has not yet come,"* Mary said to the servants, *"Do whatever he tells you,"* And thus, Jesus' mission began. Mary said "yes" again to the "hour" that would come. She said "yes" to the suffering she knew she would endure. Her suffering is shown in The Pieta by Michelangelo, which may bring you comfort by meditating on this image/sculpture.

Meditate on the passion of Jesus through the lens and heart of Mary. Mary knew the truths of all that her son would endure, the betrayal, scourging, mocking, the crown of thorns, the pain of the cross, and every nail that entered His flesh she felt reverberate in her body. And she prayed for God's Will to be done!

Many people are familiar with the story of Job. Job accepted his suffering despite being righteous and despite the fact that his wife wanted to curse God and die. Job didn't, even though he firmly believed he had done nothing wrong and was righteous in God's eyes. God allowed this trial on Job, which came with immense suffering and loss. After all the trials Job endured, God reminded Job of how small he really is in the grand scheme of things. Instead of Job being angry, he was humbled and repented — a difficult task to do.

St. Catherine of Sweden, while she did not experience a miscarriage herself, counseled many women who endured pregnancy loss. Her prayer is listed in the "Pregnancy After a Loss" section. Asking her for intercession may bring you comfort.

"Dear St. Catherine, patron of those who have suffered a miscarriage, you know the dangers that await unborn infants. Please intercede for me that I may receive healing from the loss I have suffered. My soul has been deprived of peace and I have forgotten what true happiness is. As I mourn the loss of my child, I place myself in the hands of God and ask for strength to accept His will in all things, for consolation in my grief, and for peace in my sorrow. Glorious St. Catherine, hear my prayers and ask that God, in good time, grant me a healthy baby who will become a true child of God. Amen."

St. Zelie Martin, the mother of St. Therese of Lisieux, who suffered the loss of four of her children, had this to say:

"When I closed the eyes of my dear little children and buried them, I felt sorrow through and through...People said to me, 'It would have been better never to have had them.' I couldn't stand such language. My children were not lost forever; life is short and full of miseries,

and we shall find our little ones again up above." – St. Zelie Martin

St. Gianna Beretta Molla is the patron saint of unborn children. She is a modern-day saint. During her fourth pregnancy, she was in extreme pain due to a tumor growing in her uterus alongside her baby. She was encouraged to abort the baby, as this condition is often fatal. Gianna refused to abort and endured pain and suffering while saving her baby's life. Her daughter was born; however, Gianna suffered complications following the birth and died within the week. Her death was in 1962, and she was canonized in 2004. Her husband and children, including the daughter who was saved, were present at her canonization.

These few saints are shared here to help you process your own suffering, and they can be wonderful intercessors for you. Suffering is part of our lives and always will be (see Spe Salvi 36). Even though it is very painful for us, hope is born through suffering.

> *"When no one listens to me any more, God still listens to me. When I can no longer talk to anyone or call upon anyone, I can always talk to God. When there is no longer anyone to help me deal with a need or expectation that goes beyond the human capacity for hope, he can help me. When I have been plunged into complete solitude ...; if I pray I am never totally alone."*
> *– Spe Salvi 32*

God can make great things happen through suffering if we bring this to Him. This is not about "getting over it." It's getting through it and reframing this from "I'm still hurting" to "I am accepting this cross even though I still hurt."

God will use this for good. You must keep the faith. You are resilient. Continue to pray and reach out to God even when it's hard. Even when the yoke feels heavy. It will be returned to you somehow, even if we do not recognize it. This is God's mercy.

I Have No Living Children; When Will I Have a Living Baby?

> *"Better than this is childlessness with virtue, for in the memory of virtue is immortality because it is known both by God and by men."* – Wisdom 4:1

Living childless does not mean you are not a mother. It is often hard to feel like a mother when we do not have a living child as proof of motherhood. If you feel like embracing this motherhood, don't let others take your motherhood away. You are a mother to a child who is no longer living. You cooperated with God, your Creator, in creating a new life. That life had a body and a soul. You are a mother, and your husband is a father.

> *"The most important person on earth is a mother. She cannot claim the honor of having built Notre Dame Cathedral. She need not. She has built something more magnificent than any cathedral—a dwelling for an immortal soul, the tiny perfection of her baby's body. Mothers are closer to God the Creator than any other creature: God joins force with mothers in performing this act of creation."* – Beholding Beauty, Pauline Book & Media, 2020, 106

This quote is profound. It shares the dignity you have as a mother of a child who lived for a short time. Their immortal soul still exists! Your womb was a beautiful home for your child who never knew cold or hate. Your child only knew and felt love. Accept your motherhood and encourage your husband to accept his fatherhood.

But the reality is that, sometimes, a living baby never comes. The hope that you will have a living baby should not cease. Childless Catholics face struggles in the pews as they are surrounded by screaming babies and pregnant bellies. As Catholics, we hear "Be fruitful and multiply" often, and the Catechism of the Catholic Church tells us that children are the "supreme gift of marriage." This can be very difficult, and it may bring feelings and emotions that your marriage isn't blessed.

Also, priests tend to praise large families for their obedience and fidelity to church teaching while inadvertently implying that small families, or those without children, are unfaithful. Many people assume couples with small families or childless couples are contracepting and childless by choice. This can feel like a heavy cross to bear because it is. Some begin to question God and lose sight of His divine plan. Many women feel this means they are not worthy of children, or worse, that she is cursed like the women in the Bible.

In scripture, a barren womb is perceived as a curse; however, most of the barren women in scripture were very virtuous women. For example, after arguing with her husband Elkanah, Hannah ran to the temple. There, she wept bitterly, moving her mouth with no sound. The priest, Eli, thought she was drunk and questioned her. Hannah replied that she had not been drinking but was pouring out her soul to the Lord. Eli answers, "Go in peace and may the God of Israel grant your petition which you have made to him." She immediately went away, ate, and her countenance was no longer sad.

Hannah was no longer sad after she went to the temple and prayed. She had hope that her prayer had been heard and would be answered. She went away in peace, not knowing if the outcome would be a child. She left with hope, and hope leads us to trust in God's providential plan.

God opens and closes the wombs of the women in the Bible. He opens and closes the wombs of women today. He has a purposeful intervention in the lives of those faithful to His covenant as part of His divine plan.

You are not cursed. This may be a cross, albeit a painful one. You must endure. This is easy to say but not easy to practice, especially when a close friend complains about her pregnancy discomfort. It is very easy to fall into jealousy or envy. In the Bible, Rachel and Jacob turn on each other out of envy for Leah's fertility. St. Pope John Paul II says in The Genius of Women, *"The woman has to take care that her sensitivity to others does not succumb to the temptation to possessive selfishness."*

Possessive selfishness can turn the child into a mere object of desire or commodity. We are not guaranteed children and to demand them rather than receive them as a gift strips the child of his or her dignity. It is much easier then, to idolize parenthood and succumb to the lure of assisted reproductive technologies. This field preys upon desperate parents. It can be very tempting to take one egg and one sperm and create a child in a lab through IVF.

We cannot know God's plan for us. Abraham and Sarah waited ten long years before taking things into their own hands. Ishmael was not conceived out of their love, and instead of cooperating with God's plan for them, they chose their own path. Cooperation in God's plan might require carrying the cross of childlessness, as difficult as this cross is.

> *"The LORD is good to those who wait for him, to the soul that seeks him. It is good that one should wait quietly for the salvation of the LORD."* – Lamentations 3:25-26

The Catechism of the Catholic Church says, *"Spouses to whom God has not granted children can nevertheless have a conjugal life full of meaning, in both human and Christian terms. Their marriage can radiate a fruitfulness of charity, of hospitality, and of sacrifice."* – CCC1654

Fruitfulness does not always mean children. Often, well-meaning friends and family offer adoption as the option to living childless, but adoption is not meant for every person. Discernment is necessary to determine if God is calling you to adopt. It can also be very painful to be barraged with adoption information as if you had never considered it.

> *"It is important to remember that infertile couples are fruitful when their married love is 'open to others, to the needs of the apostolate ... the needs of the poor...the needs of orphans' and to the world."* – St. John Paul II, Homily, 1982; quoted in Married Love and the Gift of Life

Couples can grow closer together in their shared suffering. Meditate on the stories of these scriptural women: Sarah, Rachel, Hannah, and Michal (since she remained childless). You and your husband grieve this together and offer this suffering together. You will gain strength together in the sacraments because of the gift of grace received in the sacraments. Attend Mass often and confession when necessary. There is much more to be said on these topics. Check the resources section for books that dive deeper into suffering.

Finally, consider the excellent novena of St. Anne and St. Joachim, the parents of the Blessed Virgin Mary who were scorned by their neighbors for their childlessness yet, in their old age, conceived.

How do I "Parent" my Deceased Child?

It's often hard to even consider this, especially when we don't feel like parents. The secular world doesn't recognize this kind of parenthood. When we have a new baby, there are outward ways to parent them, like changing diapers, rocking them, kissing them, getting up often throughout the night, etc. So how does one parent a child who is deceased?

The Dignity in a Name

This is one of the first steps a parent makes, they name their child. It doesn't matter how far along you were when you experienced this loss. You had hopes and dreams and aspirations for this baby. Some of you may have already been picking out names because that's what expecting parents do. They spend significant time considering baby names. This does not change merely because the child died.

A good name is better than precious ointment, and the day of death than the day of birth. – Ecclesiastes 7:1

You may have even found the perfect name for this child, but now that they have died, you may feel like saving this name for a living baby. While some choose to do this, this was the name you chose for this baby. Grant your child the dignity of the name you chose while he or she lived in your womb. If you do choose to save that name, give your child the honor of a name. Pray about it with your husband, and if you did not have a name chosen or have one you were considering, ask God to give you the name for this child. He will.

Some families struggle with naming their baby because they don't have confirmation about the baby's gender, and therefore choose not to name their child. One option is to find a gender-neutral name that is acceptable regardless of the sex of the baby. Other families give both a male and female name, such as Mary Joseph or Joseph Mary. Naming a child is often one of the first "acts" of parenting. You are a parent.

Once you choose your baby's name, say it! Then have your baby's name written in the book of life at your parish. This is usually done in November; however, some priests will offer this at the death of your baby.

Rituals

For many, parenting comes in the form of rituals on their due date or death date, or any other date that is significant. Some people plant a tree. Some release balloons, light a candle, pick flowers and send them down a stream. Some will take the day off and spend it in nature, attend Mass or go to adoration.

Some people also have a memorial plaque made, acquire a birthstone in the baby's honor, or donate to a charitable organization. Some organizations put together bereavement walks for pregnancy loss. They focus on bereavement care, resources, and support for those touched by different types of loss, including miscarriage, stillbirth, or neonatal death.

There are annual candlelight vigils on October 15th all over the world in honor of Pregnancy and Infant Loss Remembrance Day. Since the holidays can be a difficult time for many, some families donate to a charity in honor of their baby, participate in an Angel Tree or Adopt a Family/Child, and shop for a child that would be the same age as their baby. This can be very comforting and healing.

Participate in the Mass of the Holy Innocents (usually on December 28th). The Mass of the Holy Innocents is a remembrance of the first martyrs, the boy babies killed by Herod. Miscarried babies are typically remembered at this Mass. Sometimes there are other Masses throughout the year for miscarried or stillborn children.

Baby Book or Memory Box

With a miscarriage, there might not be many tangible items of your baby or anything your baby touched. Still, many families create a memory book and put the following items inside: positive pregnancy test, lab results, ultrasound photos, hospital band from D&C, completed journal, pictures drawn, poems, work from therapy, the birth announcement, pictures siblings made, and any sympathy cards received.

A baby book or a memory box is a great way to keep all of your essential mementos together. Some families are able to include pictures from labor and birth, along with a lock of hair. Other suitable items might be pictures or cards from your baby shower, the outfit you were planning on bringing your baby home in, your baby's hospital band, your hospital band, and handprints and/or footprints. Other items from the hospital, such as a baby blanket, can also be placed in the book or box. Some hospitals dress babies who have died. You can place your baby's clothes in the book or box.

Whatever you choose, it should feel right to you. If you're reading this as you're experiencing your loss, keep in mind that you might not be in an emotional state to make these decisions, and that's okay. If you didn't get any of these mementos or weren't given options, this may be difficult for you. Everyone will use their baby book differently. There is no right or wrong way.

Other Keepsakes

You can have virtually anything made to serve as a reminder of your baby. Stained-glass candle holders, ornaments, small blankets, weighted teddy bears (for older babies), fetal sculptures for the gestational week, art, shadow/silhouette photography (to add your baby/child to a family picture), jewelry with your baby's name/birthstone, etc. Displaying these in your home keeps your child "alive" and present daily.

Blessed are those who mourn, for they shall be comforted.
— MATTHEW 5:4

CHAPTER TEN: OTHERS WHO GRIEVE

Your Grieving Husband

While women experience both emotional and physical loss, men will only experience emotional loss. They won't experience the cramps, leaky breasts, the return of menstruation, or feel that their bodies failed. However, your husband will most likely experience some level of grief. This is an area that is often overlooked.

Some of the feelings men experience are anger, denial, helplessness, loss of control, disbelief, uselessness, and guilt. Feelings of loss and despair are common, and your husband may attempt to hide this from you. Many men also fear that their wives will die. This is common with any birth complication and is no different from pregnancy loss.

He will watch you go through an experience he may not fully understand, and it may make him uncomfortable to realize he cannot take away any of the emotional or physical pain. He may not ask questions because he does not understand medical terms or is uncomfortable. He may suppress his grief in order to support you.

You may also get frustrated with him because he may not seem to grieve. It's very common for men to grieve differently than women. Men tend to grieve more privately. It can also be very difficult for you if he wasn't attached to the pregnancy or baby. The only attachment he might have had for an early loss may have been a positive pregnancy test or an ultrasound picture. He didn't experience food cravings, nausea, or a growing belly with butterfly flicks, kicks, and punches. You may feel, at times, like you're grieving alone.

Women have reported that their husbands seemed to retreat. Many became involved in projects such as building things or fixing up the house. Some men completely sink into their work or withdraw — going in early and staying late. They might work long hours, pick up extra shifts, and seem to be avoiding the home.

Some men will outwardly mourn their loss. You may see them cry, which can be painful for you. It is also very common for men to seem stoic in the first few months following the loss, but regress three to six months later. This is due to pent-up emotions and your husband finally being able to release his grief. Society also pushes the attitude that men shouldn't cry because it shows weakness. We know this isn't true, but sometimes men suppress their feelings to fall in line with this societal attitude. In addition, men sometimes feel left out since much of the attention is placed on the woman's grief.

It is important to check in with him. He may carry a heavy burden, especially if he has been the one to share the news. Ask him questions and let him know you are there to support him as well. If this is too difficult for you as you navigate your own grief, ask someone to check in. Many fathers say it takes a long time for anyone to ask how they are doing, or they are never asked at all.

Give him specific ways he can support you. Tell him you need him to hold you, talk with you, or ask you questions about what you are experiencing. He needs to know how to help you. He may have never been through this before, and he cannot read your mind. He'll need guidance on how to help you. Also, ask him how you can help him in his grief. Maybe he needs another man to talk with, and you can help by asking your support groups or friends. Perhaps he needs space each day to be on his own, so encourage him to go to adoration or go with him to adoration. Be sure to find out what his needs are too.

Some men resort to smoking, alcohol, and drugs. This is an unhealthy way to grieve, and it is vital that you both seek counseling and assistance. It can be difficult for men to talk out these feelings, but there are many men-only groups as well as individuals who have been through miscarriage and stillbirth and are open to talking about their experiences. Online support groups are very popular for men, and there are many men-specific blogs out there too.

Your Living Children

Children grieve too. If you told your children about your pregnancy, it is best to tell them the truth about what happened. A simple explanation is that "Mommy/Daddy is crying because the baby died," which helps reduce the fear that they did something wrong or somehow caused your pain. They will ask questions, and navigating through them can be very hard. It's okay to tell them you will talk about it later.

Children are very perceptive and can tell when something is amiss, even if we try to hide it. Sometimes, it is best to grieve with them so you can show them how to recover. It helps to build resilience. The truth is always best, and you will likely find that you grow together in this grief.

If you didn't share your pregnancy with your children, they'll sense that something is wrong no matter how hard you try to hide your feelings and emotions. When children see their parents try to hide their pain, it can be very scary. They may feel they have done something wrong. They most likely have never seen you or their father this way before. It is very important to talk with them and share with them in terms they can understand. You know your child(ren) best; reveal to them what you feel is age-appropriate.

Grief in children can manifest in many ways, depending on their age. For children over the age of six, stomachaches, headaches, and disagreements in school or with friends is often how grief or confusion at home manifests. In younger children, they can begin to wet their bed or regress to wearing diapers despite being potty-trained.

Older children may feel guilty as if they caused the loss somehow. Guilt can appear regardless of whether or not they wanted a brother or sister. Even a child that said they only wanted a sister and the baby was a brother, or vice-versa, can feel guilt. It can be helpful to find group therapy or a therapist that specializes in child grief.

If you can't find the words, purchase a book. Most have storylines that are age-appropriate. They can be difficult to read because of your emotional state, but they can help put the words in your mouth that you have struggled to find.

If you're having intense feelings of guilt because you are grieving and unable to care for the home as usual, try to take some time out for your children. Be patient with yourself. You're not superwoman, and this will be a small blip on their screen years later. Playdates and time with the grandparents can help relieve some stress on you and your husband. Do your best to help them understand what you're experiencing and talk with them about what they are feeling.

Remember that this is not your fault. You did not cause this grief your child is experiencing. You do not need to move on quickly to make life return to normal for you and your family. Children will see that it is okay to grieve and mourn by watching the way you grieve and mourn. Your life will most likely never feel the same, but happiness will return. Children will see this as well, which will help them feel safe with their feelings.

Your Parents and/or In-Laws

Your parents and parents-in-law are likely to grieve in some way as well. They were anxiously awaiting the birth of their grandchild. Grandparents are lost grievers and also carry a heavy burden. They grieve the loss of their grandchild, but they are also experiencing tremendous pain because of your suffering. They want nothing but to take your pain away, and many feel helpless because they cannot take away your pain.

Many grandmothers have also experienced a pregnancy loss, which was likely hidden from you. This could bring up her own feelings of guilt or shame or immense sadness as very often they, too, were not allowed to grieve and were encouraged to forget about their baby.

This is not your fault, and you should not feel that you need to help them process their own loss(es). This section merely makes you aware that they may be grieving too, and many will want to help you through this. Allow them in where you can, such as preparing meals for you or cleaning your home.

Future Children

If or when you choose to have another baby, he or she will not replace the baby that died. You will have to decide if you want to share your pregnancy loss with your future children. The when and how you do it may vary. Some families share from the beginning. They always talk about their deceased baby; they may have pictures in their home, mementos, or other important items they share.

Some families gradually share about their deceased children, and some never share. There are also books available that can help put this experience into words. Books can be a healing way to introduce the deceased sibling to future siblings.

And we are writing this that our joy might be complete.
— 1 JOHN 1:4

CHAPTER ELEVEN: SHARING YOUR LOSS

Saying It

My baby died. My daughter passed away. I have one living child. It's hard at first and can be awkward. Being able to acknowledge what happened and say it aloud may make it more real and easier to accept. If you're afraid to tell people what happened, try not to be. It can be very healing for you to say it out loud. Encourage others to use your baby's name. If you don't feel like you need to say it, that's okay too. What's important is that you do what feels right for you.

How to Tell Your Family and Friends

You most likely have announced your pregnancy, but what do you do now that it has ended? You may feel compelled to announce your baby's death. For some, announcing the baby's death seems proper, while others want to keep it to themselves. If you are ready to share your loss, the big question is how?

Phone Calls and/or Text Messages

You may feel up to making phone calls to friends and family but enlist your husband or another close friend to do this if you don't. Choose wisely, especially if you have a friend or family member who is currently pregnant. It can be as simple as saying, "We went to the doctor today and learned our baby died. Please pray for us."

You may prefer to send a text message. Simply saying, "I had a miscarriage today," may be all that's needed. Be sure to tell them what you need from them, such as wanting them to sit with you, attend an appointment with you, prepare meals, clean the house, or just provide an ear to share your story. Use the tips below to help them help you. "Helping Someone Through Pregnancy Loss" is also found on my blog at elizabethpetrucelli.com. You could cut and paste the link into your text message.

Social Media

You might feel called to announce the miscarriage on Facebook or other social media sites. Many people simply say, "We regretfully announce that we have lost our baby to miscarriage. Please keep us in your thoughts and prayers as we grieve during this time." Some also say, "We are having another miscarriage," or "We were expecting our baby on December 7, 2015, but sadly, he was born too early this morning."

Some attach an ultrasound photo or even a photo of the baby. I will warn you, though, even though your baby is beautiful, some people will be offended seeing a picture of a baby that has died, no matter how early or full-term. Some of your Facebook "friends" may even go so far as to report the photo as graphic and request removal from

Facebook, which can hurt you deeply. In this instance, you can put "PIC IN COMMENTS" and share a picture that way.

Formal Announcement

Some women have adapted their miscarriage announcement from a standard baby announcement. You could choose an image such as an ultrasound photo or even a picture of a pregnancy test. Then find a statement. Obituaries and memorial quotes can be helpful.

If you named your baby, you may place your baby's name on the announcement, followed by your name, your husband's name, and the names of any siblings. The death date can be placed on the announcement, or you can use the conception date (if known) to the death date. The death date and birth date may be different. You can put both dates on the announcement or pick the one for you that has the most meaning.

Many women find it appropriate to send the announcement to close friends and family members. There are a lot of different ways to announce and honor your baby. If you feel compelled to make an announcement, take your time putting it together. You can have these printed at any of your local print stores, or they can be printed online. Families have also sent an email announcement or placed an obituary in the newspaper.

How Others May React

You won't be able to lean on every friend, sister, mother, or family member. This loss won't affect them the same way it's affected you, and many people have no idea how to react to this news. You will learn quickly whom you can lean on for support and whom you want to avoid. You may even be surprised by some of the people who will be there for you and find disappointment in the people you thought would be there but seemed to disappear.

It is not uncommon to lose friendships during and after pregnancy loss. It's okay to let them go for a little while. Focus on the friends who are there for you. You need support, and you can't be worried about a friend being upset with you because you're grieving. Your grief won't look like anyone else's. There is no right way to grieve. Just allow yourself to do it.

It may seem like the best person to lean on is someone who has experienced pregnancy loss; however, use caution. Not all pregnancy loss mothers feel pain in their loss, and some may not want to share their pain with you. Mothers willing to share their pain and allow you into their lives will make themselves known to you.

Family and friends may feel very uncomfortable. The death of a child isn't supposed to happen. It is not the natural order of life. Due to this internal discomfort, people often say the "wrong" things believing they are helpful. Because of this, try not to take their silence or inappropriate comments personally. Be prepared to be assertive and set boundaries. It's okay to express what you need and what you don't need. If someone makes an inappropriate comment, it's okay to tell them. Most people aren't trying to be malicious or hurtful; they just don't know what to do.

Help Them Help You

What May a Support Person Say or Do?

- LISTEN and Validate.
- Take them a meal.
- "Your baby/child mattered."
- "Your experience mattered."
- "Tell me your story."
- "I don't know what to say."
- "Who can I call for you?" (Be prepared to actually make those phone calls).
- "Be patient with yourself. Grief has no timeline."
- "Don't feel guilty because you laughed today."
- "Can I take your baby's siblings to the park? I know you don't feel like laughing or playing right now."
- "I am going to the store. What can I bring back for you?"
- "Talk to me. I am here to listen."
- "I am out running errands. Is there anything you need?"
- "How are you doing today?"
- "You don't have to answer the phone or call me back — I just wanted to check in on you."
- "How about I take your baby's siblings to school, or Grandma's, or ____?"
- "I would love to attend a support group or go to church with you."

What a Support Person Should Not Say

- "You can have another baby."
- "At least you know you can get pregnant."
- "It was God's way of protecting you from ____."

- "It was God's will."
- "Heaven needed another angel."
- "Your baby is better in Heaven."
- "Time heals all wounds."
- "I know just how you feel." (Unless you have personally experienced pregnancy loss).
- "It could have been worse."
- "Now you have an angel/saint in Heaven."
- "You should be over this by now! It's been ____ weeks/months/years."
- "God never gives us more than we can handle."
- "What can I do for you?" Instead, say, "Can I do ____ for you?" Or "I am going to bring over a meal." not "Can I bring over a meal?"

How a Support Person Can Help You

- Listening. You may want to talk over and over again about the pregnancy and the death experience. Finding someone who will listen no matter how many times you need to share is important. Most people want to stop listening after the third or fourth time.
- Bring tissues.
- Pray with you.
- Hug you.
- Call a priest for you.
- Encourage you to have pictures taken with your baby.
- Ask and hold your baby.
- Be a shoulder to cry on. If you don't want to talk, you may just want someone to lean on while you cry.
- Cry with you. They don't have to be stoic. Crying helps validate that this is a sad time and an experience worth grieving.

- Be there... for the birth, that is. If they would have most likely been there for the birth anyway, be sure to let them know you would still like them to be there to support you. At the very least, you may prefer they wait in the waiting room.
- Call your baby by name, which may seem weird at first. This is the preferred method unless you do not want them to call your baby by name.
- Mementos — bring something for you to remember your baby by. For any birth, people give gifts. This is no different, although the gifts might be slightly different. You may want an **outfit**. Families are often encouraged to dress their babies just like they would if the baby was born alive. A **teddy bear** that is at least 14 inches but less than 24 inches is best as well. You can hold the bear as you leave the hospital. If you provide the baby's weight, a friend can make a bear of the same weight. Anything with the **baby's name** or **birthstone** on it, such as **jewelry,** is also customary. **Cards** are also welcome and can be kept as a keepsake. Any traditional keepsakes will also work, such as something to **preserve a lock of hair, handprints/footprints, moulds,** and **books** or **special boxes** to keep pictures in.
- Have them make phone calls for you.
- Have a Mass said for you and/or your baby.
- They can send a card. Hallmark and other card makers have a line of cards for pregnancy and infant loss.
- Be comfortable in your tears.
- Attend the funeral/memorial service.
- Send a daily message without expecting a response. "How are you today?"
- Thinking of you." "Hope things are going okay."

- Understand that the next year will be a "year of firsts." Going into your home without your baby will be a "first," returning to work will be a "first," going to the same grocery store will be a "first," and any holiday will be a "first" holiday without your baby. There will be many "firsts."
- Remember the baby's birthday/saint date/death date. Send a card, make a phone call, send a text. It can be as simple as "Remembering your baby's (can insert baby's name) birth today."
- Remember the baby's due date. If your baby died before the due date, this will be a particularly difficult day. They can let you know they are thinking of you and are there for you.
- Be supportive in the weeks and months to come.
- Attend memorial events. Be there for the funeral or any memorial events, and find local walks and other annual remembrance events to help share and remember your baby.
- Set up a meal train/calendar of people who will bring you meals. Soups can be hearty and healthy. It's extremely helpful to bring veggie trays, fruit trays, sandwich trays, or just set out some healthy food. It is a reminder that you need to eat, which is often put on hold while mourning.
- Bring household items such as milk, eggs, butter, toilet paper, paper towels, paper plates, aluminum foil, toothpaste, etc.
- Mow the lawn, take out the trash, bring in the trash cans, etc.
- Pick up around the house (do laundry, mow the lawn, empty and load the dishwasher, make the beds, etc). **They should not break down the baby's nursery or remove any items for the baby.**

I will not leave you desolate; I will come to you.
—JOHN 14:18

CHAPTER TWELVE: OTHER THINGS TO CONSIDER

Baby Samples, Magazines, Registries, and More

If you signed up for baby samples, pregnancy magazines, baby registries, or other free items, you will receive items for months, and possibly years, following your loss. Some women don't have to sign up online because their doctor's office will sign them up at the first prenatal visit.

Unfortunately, many of these companies share your information, so the news spreads. You soon find yourself with stacks of samples and magazines and an email box full of mail telling you all about the development of your baby next week. These can be hurtful reminders of what was lost.

If you remember where you signed up, you can return to the website and unsubscribe. If you don't know, it may be best to enlist your husband, friend, or family member to assist you in calling the companies or fishing through your emails to unsubscribe to all these reminders. At the bottom of the email, you will find an area that says something similar to "to unsubscribe, click here." By clicking that link, you will either be unsubscribed or directed to enter the email address you would like unsubscribed. Any coupons, formula, or other baby items you receive can be donated in honor of your baby.

Medical Bills

Some insurance companies also only cover prenatal services while pregnant. If you are pending a miscarriage or require care for pregnancy loss, you may see higher copays or medical bills. This is another painful reminder of your loss.

If your baby was born in a hospital, there are usually separate bills for your baby. These medical or hospital bills come in several weeks and even months after the loss. If you choose testing or an autopsy, a bill is usually sent for these procedures. These, too, are often very painful reminders. If you used urgent care or an outpatient surgery center, they also bill. If your husband can pay those upfront, this may help alleviate reliving those memories. You can also contact your insurance companies or the doctors and ask them to send the bills addressed to your husband only.

Journaling

Journaling can help in many ways. It's a very easy way to process your experience. Many women journal in a blog or word processing program, but if you prefer, you can write in a nice journal book or any old notebook. Go with what feels good to you. You can journal each day, several times a day, or only once a week. It doesn't matter how often you journal. When you must deal with something difficult, your journal can be a companion to you.

There is no right or wrong way to journal. You can journal about the happy moments as well as the sad ones.

You can journal about what your baby may look like. You can even draw your baby and make that part of your journal. Your journal can be filled with letters to your baby, or you can talk about the medical aspects of your loss and any other struggles you're having. Your journal can hold whatever needs to be released. Journaling also helps to take some of the pressure off your husband. While your husband most likely wants to help you, he may not want to hear the story over and over again.

Therapy

It can be very helpful to find a good therapist or support group. Many support groups are free. You can find a support group at your local hospital or online at therapy centers. Attending a support group can help you validate your own grief. Some groups are large, and others are small, but it is important that you find a group that fits your needs. Some women do not want to attend a group where women share their loss stories at every session. If this concerns you, check with the group leader to see how they manage story sharing and if there are healing activities and other discussions when processing loss.

If you are concerned about your emotional state and feel "crazy," or have been told you need to seek professional help, there are many therapists who specialize in grief. It is also important to find a therapist you like and who meshes with you. You may be able to find recommendations from support group members, other friends, and family or by calling local support organizations in your area. Some spiritual direction from your priest may also help.

Mother's Day

It's hard for most women to believe they're mothers if they have no living children. You conceived a child in your womb and did all the right things for that child. You prayed for that child's health, and you may feel guilty thinking that you did something that may have caused this. Your baby didn't die because of anything you did. Still, it doesn't change the fact that you had a child, and that child died. Celebrate Mother's Day in whatever way feels right for you, and pray for the Blessed Mother to comfort you.

Father's Day

This can be a difficult day for him as well. Check in with him. He is a father as well and might appreciate the recognition. Celebrate Father's Day in the way it feels right. It could be as simple as a card, a walk together, an adoration together, a rosary together, or even an elaborate family dinner.

Fear not, for I am with you, be not dismayed, for I am your God; I will strengthen you, I will help you, I will uphold you with my victorious right hand. – ISAIAH 41:10

CHAPTER THIRTEEN: RE-ENTERING SOCIETY

After experiencing miscarriage, when it's time to go to the store, go back to work, or just go out, there may be reminders of the pregnancy everywhere. Going to Mass can be especially difficult because many parishioners might have known you were pregnant. You may have had a growing belly, and now your belly is flat or flabby. Being prepared for how to handle these encounters is important.

When a person asks and discovers you are no longer pregnant, they may also feel devastated for you. It is not your responsibility to make them feel better or comfort them. You cannot control their feelings, so try not to feel guilty for sharing your story.

Time Off for Miscarriage

It is important that you take time away from work for as long as you can and as long as you feel you need to. Talk with your employer and request as much time off as possible.

Depending on your employer, time off for a miscarriage may be covered under FMLA (Family Medical Leave Act);

however, keep in mind that FMLA does not necessarily mean you will have paid time off. Some employers allow sick time and/or vacation time to provide a paycheck during FMLA. Check with your human resources department to determine your employer's policy.

In addition, the requested time off under FMLA would not be recognized as time off due to the birth of a child. The most common condition that has been accepted for time off due to miscarriage is defined by FMLA as a:

"Serious health condition" which means an illness, injury, impairment, or physical or mental condition that involves: "a period of incapacity requiring absence of more than three calendar days from work, school, or other regular daily activities that also involves continuing treatment by (or under the supervision of) a health medical provider."

You will need to work with a therapist or medical provider to complete the necessary paperwork to take this time off and be protected by FMLA. Your husband may also qualify and file for FMLA. Have him check with his human resources department.

Note on Bereavement Leave:
You may want bereavement leave as you lost a child and may need to plan a funeral or make other arrangements; however, most companies do not give parents bereavement for miscarriage or stillbirth. They should allow you to take FMLA or PTO, but their bereavement policy may "require" a "living child" outside the womb. This can be a painful reality.

Even though you may be experiencing the emotional anguish that follows pregnancy loss, you must keep in mind that you have just given birth, and your body will need time to recover. If you don't feel comfortable taking time off because of your emotional or mental state, it is perfectly acceptable to request time off due to the healing your body needs.

You may be bleeding and cramping for several days or longer. If you had given birth at full-term, you would need at least two to four weeks to recover from birth. You may also lactate (make breast milk) even in an early miscarriage. Every woman's body is different and responds differently. You may go through the same emotional roller coaster that women experience following a full-term birth.

Remember, every pregnant woman, regardless of whether or not her baby is born alive or not, needs time to heal. Your body has produced hormones and has adjusted in ways we don't fully understand or know. Your body can't go back to a pre-pregnant state immediately.

In addition, many work situations are not accommodating to regular crying spells, so it is recommended that you wait to go back until you're past the early weepy stages of postpartum hormonal changes and grief. Be kind to yourself. Grief is hard, and it can take a long time to feel normal again.

Going to Mass

It is important you return to Mass as soon as you physically can, even if emotionally you are weepy. This can be a triggering experience. Bring tissues. Prepare your husband to intervene if/when questions are asked. Your husband's vocation is to protect you, so allow him this opportunity to love you the way Christ loves you. Some women arrive early to avoid seeing too many people that may ask questions or see their tears. If you arrive early, pray the rosary with your husband and/or family.

Staying after Mass to socialize may not be comforting, although some women have taken this time to share their stories with church friends and acquaintances. Be open to anything. You may decide before Mass you will stay, but after Mass, you may feel the need to run. Regardless of what you choose, God wants you to receive Him in the Holy Eucharist.

Please note:
Anger is a normal part of the grief process. CCC 2302 explains anger and what may be considered sinful anger. When anger leads us to a vindictive attitude, this leads us into sin, and we should seek the Sacrament of Penance/Reconciliation before receiving the Eucharist. This is a time when you need the sacraments the most. Try not to be scrupulous and seek out your priest if you are concerned your anger is mortal. Many priests offer confession before Mass begins. If you cannot participate in confession prior to Mass, please withhold from receiving the Eucharist until you have gone to confession.

Going Back to Work

You may need to take some time planning how you might deal with any questions or hurtful comments from coworkers, clients, students, or others whom you interact with at work. One of the most common ways to share your news is via email or letter. You can send a scripted letter/email or have your supervisor send out the message.

Be sure you check your company policy to ensure you are not violating a policy, as some employers do not allow you to send out mass emails. The message should be short but explain the situation and include how you feel now. This will help your co-workers understand where you are in your journey and how to help you at that stage. You could even include the list of what to say and not to say in your message.

It's okay for you to educate people about how their comments can be more helpful. You can be very specific and let people know that comments such as, "I am so sorry for your loss. I am here for you" are appreciated. Let them know you may just need to talk or cry, and it's okay that they just listen and not try to fix things.

You can also let them know what not to say, such as, "You can always have another," or "It was God's plan," or "It's nature's way of dealing with a sick baby," or "You already have a child and should feel blessed." Sometimes people say those things, trying to make you feel better, but in the end, those comments usually do more harm than good. It's appropriate for you to let people know that. See Chapter Eleven for more information.

Remember that these comments aren't meant to be hurtful. Situations like this make others uncomfortable. Miscarriage is very common, but many women are left to grieve in silence. You might be surprised to learn that your friend or co-worker also had a loss.

Going back at the end of the workweek instead of the beginning has also shown to be very helpful. This gives you that "light at the end of the tunnel" feeling where you know that you only have a day or so until the weekend when you can recover. Scheduling self-care for that first weekend is also essential. A massage, mani/pedi, date night, night out with friends, or a night in with a warm blanket and a special movie can help you feel better after a stressful week at work.

Going Out in Public

It is inevitable. You will have to go out in public at some point. Some people may have known that you were pregnant and will either ask you how the baby is or how the pregnancy is going or notice that your belly has gotten smaller. Having a canned response can be very helpful during these encounters. Many women feel more comfortable with those first few outings when they have a friend or someone with them to help deflect the comments or step in should emotions take over.

As you navigate the public again, you will one day be asked how many children you have or if you plan on having any children. Some women share their stories of loss with others easily, yet others struggle to communicate. Sometimes random strangers have a difficult time understanding, and the roles change when the grieving parent feels they need to comfort and reassure the stranger.

Finding balance in whom you share and what you share will be helpful. It's okay not to tell every person you come in contact with, just as it's perfectly fine to tell every person you come in contact with. Some women like to practice what they will say ahead of time and have found that it makes encounters less awkward. It is also important to be kind to yourself if you don't share your experience with your child and begin to feel guilty. You may not always share your child, and that's okay. If you find you are feeling guilty about this, writing a letter to your child can help, or sharing your story the next time you are out.

Others Who Are Pregnant

You will cross paths with other pregnant women, even within your close family. This can be difficult as you navigate your new normal. You might be expected to put on a baby shower or, at the very least, attend a baby shower. If it doesn't feel right, it is important not to do it. Don't push yourself to be there for someone else. Talk with this pregnant mother and share your feelings. She may not understand, but your emotional health is more important.

Trust your gut and stay home if that's what feels right. You may also notice that your pregnant friends stop sharing their pregnancy news. Many do this because they don't want to hurt you. They are unsure of what to do or say. If it bothers you, share those feelings as well.

Many loss mothers temporarily remove themselves from social media sites to get a reprieve from all the baby announcements, pregnancy complaints, and pictures of new babies. It's okay to remove yourself. When it feels right, you can pick up where you left off.

Cast all your anxieties on him, for he cares about you."
— 1 PETER 5:7

CHAPTER FOURTEEN: PREGNANCY AFTER LOSS

What to expect with pregnancy following a miscarriage is important. Fear of enduring another miscarriage is one of the biggest concerns. While you may feel more prepared than ever if you experience another loss, you may still be hurting deeply from your previous loss and fear the experience of suffering again. God has entrusted you with this child, no matter how long you have with this new creation, so if you find yourself pregnant after a loss, praise God for this gift and try to find joy.

Many factors must be taken into consideration when deciding to try again.

Discernment

"Ask and it will be given to you; seek, and you will find, knock and it will be opened to you. For everyone who asks receives, and he would seeks finds, and to him who knocks, it will be opened." – Matthew 7:7-8

Always ask God first. Go to adoration, sit in front of the Blessed Sacrament, and ask God to help guide you. It's best you and your husband go together. If your husband won't go with you or pray with you, encourage him to go to adoration alone. God will often reveal pieces to each of you to put together, but if you do not ask, you will not receive.

Have open communication and talk with each other about your feelings. If your miscarriage was scary and there were complications, he may not be ready. Pray together and often. Saying the rosary together with the intention of "reveal Your Will to us for our family" can be very helpful. You may find obstacles in your way and make excuses, so you will need to work together, along with God, to overcome these obstacles.

Talk with a trusted priest and do not accept advice from the priest that says contraception is needed to avoid pregnancy. Contraception is never okay. If you must avoid pregnancy for a time, abstinence is necessary. A priest can provide you with prayers, more information on discernment, pray for you and offer up your suffering as well.

This discernment might cause you anxiety and grief. There is no rush to have a baby. Take things slowly and in prayer. Bring this heavy burden to the Cross and lay it at Jesus' feet. Literally stand or kneel in front of a crucifix or the Blessed Sacrament. Say, "Jesus, I do not want to worry about this anymore. I am laying this at the foot of your cross to do with as you will." Or, ask Him to help you through this and help you know by sending you a sign that you cannot doubt.

Is Your Body Physically Ready?

Talk with your medical provider to ensure your body has healed and can carry another child. Seeking a NaPro

Technology practitioner may be very beneficial to you as they work with you to correct any menstrual and fertility conditions to improve your procreative potential. They will not offer you assisted reproductive technologies that are inconsistent with Church teaching.

Most medical providers recommend that you experience a few menstrual cycles before attempting another pregnancy. Studies show; however, that you are most fertile in the three months following a miscarriage[14]. You will also need a plan on how to avoid pregnancy if your doctor recommends delaying pregnancy, you don't feel ready, or you have been told another pregnancy could be fatal for you.

If you and your husband decide one or both of you aren't ready, that is okay. You may also discern this with your priest. Church teaching prohibits contraception of any form. This situation does not make contraception medically necessary. Please do not jeopardize your soul by using condoms, birth control pills, or an IUD (intrauterine device). Abstinence is the only licit (approved) option during this time.

Abstinence can be difficult for one or both of you. Often couples need to feel the marital embrace at this difficult time. Pray together. Offer this up for the souls in purgatory. You have an opportunity to save souls; don't miss it. Someone needs you.

If you are feeling very drawn to each other sexually, it may be a prompting from the Holy Spirit that you should come together in the marital embrace. Trust in God's Will for you and accept His design. You may be surprised at what He has in store for you. Keep in mind that pregnancy is not a consequence of sex. You may or may not conceive.

Am I Emotionally Ready?

Having another baby won't take away the sadness or grief you experience because of your loss. Some women may feel more guilt because they conceived again. This guilt may stem from feeling like you haven't grieved the loss completely. Maybe it feels like you are attempting to replace the baby, or perhaps because you conceived too soon. These are all normal feelings.

You can write a letter to your new baby or the baby who passed and explain your feelings. This can be very therapeutic. Putting your thoughts on paper and re-reading them can help make sense of them. Most of all, having another baby won't make the baby who died any less loved. By being open to life, you are participating in God's plan. You are giving your child(ren) a brother or sister, and you are adding souls to the world!

When You Become Pregnant Again

Praise be to God! Amid the fear of this happening again, we must not forget to thank Him for this new gift! Offer your worries to God in the same way you offered up your suffering. You may also have doubts about your medical provider or insurance company. It's important to find a medical provider you can trust.

If you have the option of "shopping" for a medical provider, search for one that understands pregnancy after a loss. Reveal your prior loss(es) to them and see if they offer extra testing, more frequent appointments, or other support you feel you will need this time around. This will build trust in their abilities and build trust in yourself as you search for a medical provider for you and your baby.

You may also worry about this pregnancy. Many women experience anxiety during their subsequent pregnancies and then become concerned that this worry could be passed onto the new baby during gestation. Try to focus on all the positive things taking place and acknowledge the wonder and awe of this current pregnancy. This baby is a new creation and God has entrusted this new child to you!

You may find it helpful to share the news of your pregnancy with trusted friends and family members so you have people you can count on for support when you're overly anxious. Having at least one person you know you can rely on can help reduce any anxiety. Sometimes; however, your husband cannot be that other person. Sometimes they, too, are overly anxious. They may be wondering where the "safe spot" in pregnancy is so they can "stop worrying."

Focus on lowering your stress level. Exercise can be extremely beneficial. Pregnancy exercise classes help with breathing and building strength. Many people can do pregnancy exercise classes. In addition, eat right and take time for yourself. Now could be the time to start regular pregnancy massages, prayer devotions, and other stress-reducing habits. Another idea to help with bonding and reduce stress is to take a bath each day (but get out of the bath if you start overheating to avoid overheating the baby).

It is a rare person who takes time each day to focus on reducing anxiety. Your husband can help by setting up the bathtub. Dim the lights, light some candles, turn on some soft music, and relax in the warmth of the water. Rub your belly and talk to your baby. Really listen to your body and send positive messages to your baby. Offer prayers for this baby. This will help counteract all the anxiety and negativity you have been feeling. For this moment, you are loving on your baby.

Despite the uncertainty, bonding with your baby is essential. It might be hard, but you must try for the baby's sake. Write a positive note to your baby daily and pray for them. Collect these notes of positivity and love. If you fear bonding because of guilt, understand that nothing will replace the baby you lost. Each baby is a unique creation by God.

"Oh, everlasting and Almighty God, who, through the operation of the Holy Spirit, did prepare the body and soul of the glorious Virgin Mary, Mother of God, to be a worthy dwelling for Thy Son, and who, through the same Holy Spirit, did sanctify Saint John the Baptist before his birth; deign to hear the prayer of thy humble servant. I implore Thee, through the intercession of Saint Gerard, to protect me in motherhood and to safeguard against the evil spirit the child which Thou has given me, that by Thy saving Hand, it may receive Holy Baptism. Grant also that, having lived as Christians on earth, we may attain to everlasting bliss in heaven. Through the same Christ our Lord. Amen." – The Prayer Book, Catholic Press (1954)

So you have sorrow now, but I will see you again and your hearts will rejoice, and no one will take your joy from you."
– JOHN 16:22

CHAPTER FIFTEEN: IMAGO DEI (In His Image)

The dignity of the human person from conception to natural death is a phrase often heard among Catholics. This is a dignity that you cannot gain or lose, it is given by God, it is inherent. Yet the current culture defines who has value and how much. The current culture doesn't value life in general and, therefore, doesn't value the unborn.

When it comes to providing a worldly view of dignity, it is compassion and care. Very few of us truly understand how to provide dignity to the unborn when they die in the womb. The information in this book gives that guidance. Imagine the graces that could flow if more of us, including the clergy within the church, understood how to provide that dignity.

When we treat others with dignity, we love. When we love, we serve God. When we serve God in the way he commands us, we can receive everlasting life. Death, therefore, isn't the end. Death is the beginning of eternal happiness with our Father in Heaven…as he destined for us. Unfortunately for us, many babies will receive eternal happiness before we had a chance to enjoy them here on this earth, but we can show others how much we loved them through outward signs; proper burial, a proper name, and some other options in this book.

Much suffering can come from the fact that the babies and, for that matter, women enduring miscarriage were not treated with any dignity (care and compassion). Babies who were not or could not be baptized were not named, were flushed, or their ashes worn as jewelry. In many cases, it was a lack of knowledge. This is not meant to cause anyone pain or make anyone feel judged. If this is your circumstance, pray for a name and name your baby. Bury their ashes as prescribed.

The secular world provides little. Remember, we are not made for this world. We are merely living in it.

> *"If you were of the world, the world would love its own; but because you are not of the world, but I chose you out of the world, therefore the world hates you."* –
> John 15:19

The world is full of medical providers who don't believe in the dignity of the human person. The fact that you do and the fact that you ask them to help in providing that dignity may cause some suffering or the feeling of persecution. You have the right to demand dignity for your baby.

When the miscarriage experience is medical only, no one sheds a tear. No one recognizes the pain of the loss, and women are left confused. Women and their husbands are torn. Society says this is no big deal and to move on, yet the human heart says otherwise.

Babies who are "inside babies only" are often mistreated, tossed in the trash, buried in the backyard, or placed in planters on the porch, and are not given names because

"If we name it, it must mean something." Therefore, their remains require proper care. The women living with a deceased child in their womb or have suffered through the experience of birthing their very tiny babies, too often do not receive the recognition of birth, motherhood, or any validation that their loss is painful.

Doctors and medical personnel tell women that this happens often, there's nothing to be done, and it's best to try again. This implies that we should forget about the baby who died, forget about the love we had for that child, and that our love was put in the wrong place. It implies that the love we had for that baby was wasted. Wasted, because the baby wasn't real, the baby didn't live, or there was "something wrong with it."

The pregnancy and baby are reduced to a reproductive act instead of procreation. Humans don't reproduce, they procreate. This is just another way to dehumanize this experience. Using the term "reproduce" places humans on the same level as animals. It reduces our dignity!

> *"So God created man in his own image, in the image of God he created him."* – Genesis 1:27

God created us Imago Dei, in His Image. Humans were created in the image of the Divine. Therefore, we possess inherent dignity! What human gets to decide which humans deserve dignity? Any human that does this, including medical providers, deifies themselves. They are placing themselves as an equal to God or, worse, superior!

God is the only one who decides the dignity of the human person. God deemed the human creation "very good," which means we all have this dignity. There are no specific traits or qualities listed. Human is the trait.

At conception, we are human. A tiny zygote is "very good." An embryo is "very good." A fetus is "very good." Unborn humans, therefore, are "very good" and have the same dignity as every other person. Because our worth is connected to our Creator, humans are of immense value, even the tiny baby within the womb. They should be treated with the utmost respect from conception until their natural death.

When anyone dehumanizes a baby, it hurts. That hurt can bring on suffering. That suffering can complicate our grief. We cannot escape suffering in this world, and in fact, we should not do everything possible to eliminate suffering. We must have a better understanding of suffering and how to use our suffering for the good of others. Where there is love, there is grief, and how we treat others, including the very tiny baby in the womb, shows us just how much we love and value God.

> *"Truly, I say to you, as you did it to one of the least of these my brethren, you did it to me."* – Matthew 25:40.

Deo Gratias!

May God give us peace in our sorrow, consolation in our grief and strength to accept his will in all things.

Author Bio

Elizabeth Petrucelli is an author, certified childbirth educator, bereavement doula, and parenting instructor. She has authored *All That is Seen and Unseen – A Journey Through a First Trimester Miscarriage*, *The First Night; Small Town Fumblings of a Rookie Police Officer*, and *It's Not "Just" a Heavy Period; The Miscarriage Handbook*. Elizabeth is also the creator of The Miscarriage App; a phone application which provides support to women enduring miscarriage. Two of Elizabeth's books are utilized by hospitals, OBGYN clinics, and non-profit organizations.

Elizabeth is an active blogger at her website and has published articles in the *International Doula* and *The Mighty*. She has been a guest blogger at the Doula Spot and Cord. Elizabeth has been featured as a speaker several times on Colorado Catholic Radio Network and as a guest speaker on Whole Mother Radio, Denver Natural Mom, The Institute for Birth, Breath, and Death, Blog Talk Radio — Dunamas Center Ministries, and For Women Over 40. She has also presented at the International Childbirth Educators Association Annual Conference (2016) and has been a guest lecturer at Denver Health Hospital and Arapahoe Community College. She was also featured on 7 News Denver - Viral Video of Couples Miscarriage Sheds Light on One Taboo Topic.

Growing up in a suburb of South Tulsa, Oklahoma, Elizabeth always wanted to write a book. She often wrote short stories throughout her school years and excelled in her college English classes. After experiencing her first miscarriage, her dream of becoming an author was fulfilled after she self-published her first book *All That is Seen and Unseen; A Journey Through a First Trimester Miscarriage.*

Elizabeth is a subject matter expert, having experienced two miscarriages herself. After publishing her first book, Elizabeth became the first certified bereavement doula in the State of Colorado and began her bereavement ministry, Dragonflies for Ruby; which provided free support to families enduring pregnancy loss. She has hosted support groups for families who have experienced miscarriage as well as support groups for medical personnel who assisted families during miscarriage and stillbirth. As a bereavement doula., she has served hundreds of families through miscarriage and stillbirth. She has over 75 hours of specialized training in pregnancy loss and bereavement support.

Elizabeth hosts training workshops around the country for doulas, nurses, and other professionals on supporting women through pregnancy loss and assists OBGYN clinics in design changes and considerations for those experiencing pregnancy loss. She participated in a focus group for the National Perinatal Association and served an integral role in creating Interdisciplinary Guidelines for Care of Women Presenting to the Emergency Department with Pregnancy Loss; which was published in the Journal of Perinatalogy in 2017 and is used in hospital emergency rooms nationwide. Elizabeth also holds the Psychological First Aid (PFA) certification and is trained in Crisis Intervention and Suicide Prevention (ASIST).

Elizabeth is a former U.S. Marine, who, upon honorable discharge, began working as an administrative assistant. After the birth of her first child, Elizabeth became a labor doula, running a successful practice for over eight years. She desired a career in law enforcement and began working towards that goal. She worked in the law enforcement and security field for approximately 10 years before becoming a childbirth educator after the birth of her third child. She is a stay-at-home mom and homeschool's her children.

Elizabeth is the Founder of the Catholic Women's Conference of Denver, a non-profit organization recognized by the Archdiocese of Denver, that brings an annual conference to Catholic women across the Front Range. She also holds a Certificate in Biblical Studies from the Denver Catholic Biblical School after completing the four-year program and holds a certificate in Catholic Bioethics. She is currently in a two-year Catechetical School. She lives in Colorado with her husband of over 25 years and their three living children. She is currently working on the manuscript *Understanding and Teaching Unexpected Outcomes; A Birth Professionals Guide*.

Resources

Books for Her

After Miscarriage: A Catholic Woman's Companion to Healing & Hope by Karen Edmisten

Miscarriage: Women Sharing From the Heart by Marie Allen

Empty Arms: Coping With Miscarriage, Stillbirth and Infant Death by Sherokee Ilse

I Never Held You: Miscarriage, Grief, Healing and Recovery by Ellen M. DuBois

Books for Him

Father in Crisis: The Invisible Child by Burt Wilber

A Guide for Father's When a Baby Dies by Tim Nelson

Books for Couples

Grieving Parents: Surviving Loss as a Couple by Nathalie Himmelrich

Books for Children

Something Happened: A Book for Children and Parents Who Have Experienced Pregnancy Loss by Cathy Blanford

Someone Came Before You by Pat Schwiebert

Books for Grandparents

A Grandparent's Sorrow by Pat Schwiebert

For Bereaved Grandparents by Margaret Gerner

Books on Redemptive Suffering

Sweet Cross: A Marian Guide to Suffering by Laura Mary Phelps

Manual for Suffering by Jeffrey Kirby

Suffering: The Catholic Answer: The Cross of Christ and Its

Meaning for You by Hubert van Zeller

Salvifici Doloris – Apostolic Letter, Pope John Paul II

Miscarriage Kits and Caskets

Trappist Caskets – trappistcaskets.com/infant/
Heavens Gain – heavensgain.org

Bibliography

1. "Miscarriage: MedlinePlus Medical Encyclopedia." U.S. National Library of Medicine. U.S. National Library of Medicine, Web. 16 Jan. 2015. http://www.nlm.nih.gov/medlineplus/ency/article/001488.htm

2. "Molar Pregnancy – American Pregnancy Association." American Pregnancy Association. 26 Apr. 2012. Web. 17 Jan. 2015. http://americanpregnancy.org/pregnancy-complications/molar-pregnancy/

3. Ultrasound Obstet Gynecol 2012;40: 630 – 635. Published online in Wiley Online Library(wileyonlinelibrary.com).DOI:10.1002/uog.12277   https://obgyn.onlinelibrary.wiley.com/doi/10.1002/uog.12277

4. Transvaginal sonography in the evaluation of normal early pregnancy: Correlation with HCG level : American Journal of Ro entgenology : Vol. 153, no. 1 (AJR)   RL Bree, M Edwards, M Bohm-Velez, S Beyler, J Roberts and EB Mendelson, https://www.ajronline.org/doi/10.2214/ajr.153.1.75

5. Nanda, Kavita. "Expectant Care versus Surgical Treatment for Miscarriage." The Cochrane Database of Systematic Reviews, U.S. National Library of Medicine, 14 Mar. 2012, pubmed.ncbi.nlm.nih.gov/22419288/

6. The National Catholic Bioethics Center. "The Management of Ectopic Pregnancy." February 2013 https://www.ncbcenter.org/resources-and-statements-cms/summary-ectopic-pregnancy?rq=ectopic%20pregnancy PDF Download

7. Mavrelos, D., Memtsa, M., Helmy, S. et al. β-hCG resolution times during expectant management of tubal ectopic pregnancies. BMC Women's Health 15, 43 (2015). https://doi.org/10.1186/s12905-015-0200-7

8. Karanth L, Jaafar SH, Kanagasabai S, Nair NS, Barua A. Anti-D administration after spontaneous miscarriage for preventing Rhesus alloimmunisation. Cochrane Database Syst Rev. 2013 Mar 28;(3):CD009617. doi: 10.1002/14651858.CD009617.pub2. PMID: 23543581

9. Leever, M., Deegan-Krause, B., Leliaert, Fr R., et al . "Baptizing" Deceased Infants. Journal of the Catholic Health Association of the United States (Nov-Dec 2004)

10. Congregation for the Doctrine of the Faith, Instruction on Respect for Human Life in its Origin and on the Dignity of Procreation Donum Vitae: (1987) www.vatican.va/roman_curia/congregations/cfaith/documents/ rc_con_cfaith_doc_19870222_respect-for-human-life_en.html

11. Hamel, R. Some Guidance on Disposition of Fetal Remains. https://www.chausa.org/docs/default-source/hceusa/800560da9f7b48e390a4e89b32aaf4371-pdf.pdf?sfvrsn=2

12. Meaney, Joseph. "Bioethics and the Dignity of the Human Body." The National Catholic Bioethics Center, The National Catholic Bioethics Center, 29 Jan. 2021, www.ncbcenter.org/messages-from-presidents/dignityofthehumanbody-pj5jh?rq=autopsy

13. INTERNATIONAL THEOLOGICAL COMMISSION, The Hope of Salvation for Infants Who Die Without Being Baptised, Vatican City, 2007

14. Trying to Conceive After an Early Pregnancy Loss: An Assessment on How Long Couples Should Wait. Karen C. Schliep, Emily M. Mitchell, Sunni L. Mumford, Rose G. Radin, Shvetha M. Zarek, Lindsey Sjaarda, and Enrique F. Schisterman. Obstetrics & Gynecology. 2016 Jan 7. doi: 10.1097/AOG.0000000000001159. https://www.nih.gov/news-events/nih-research-matters/trying-to-conceive-after-pregnancy-loss

ACKNOWLEDGEMENTS

I cannot acknowledge by name all the many people who have helped me in the creation of this book, there are simply too many and I am thankful for all of them.

I thank the many priests who helped me research the liturgy, rites, and especially limbo; including my pastor and spiritual director. The priests were a combination of Novus Ordo, FSSP, and TLM priests.

To the two theologians that helped ensure my theology was correct and in-line with the Magesterium, I am forever grateful. You were kind and loving in your criticism.

To my husband and family who had to suffer through my bitterness and frustrations. I love all of you so much.

To Our Blessed Mother, who I know prompted me to write this book and who prayed for me to have the patience needed to wait; especially after my pastor asked me to make changes as the book was about to be published (delaying the publication a few months). It was for my good as well as the good of this book.

I thank God, who I owe every single breath. This book is ultimately for His Glory to bring as many souls to Him as possible. Without the grace He provided me, this book never would have come to fruition.

OTHER BOOKS BY ELIZABETH PETRUCELLI

All That is Seen and Unseen; A Journey Through a First Trimester Miscarriage

The First Night: Small Town Fumblings of a Rookie Police Officer

It's Not 'Just' a Heavy Period: The Miscarriage Handbook

Visit elizabethpetrucelli.com for more!!

www.ingramcontent.com/pod-product-compliance
Lightning Source LLC
Chambersburg PA
CBHW072050290426
44110CB00014B/1617